# FAITH IN STRUGGLE

# FAITH IN STRUGGLE

*The Protestant Churches in Nicaragua and their Response to the Revolution*

David Haslam

EPWORTH PRESS

*British Library Cataloguing in Publication Data*

Haslam, David
Faith in struggle: the Protestant Churches in Nicaragua and their response to the revolution.
1. Protestant churches—Nicaragua
I. Title
280′.4′097285 BX4834.N5

ISBN 0–7162–0436–3

First published in 1987
by Epworth Press
Room 195, 1 Central Buildings,
Westminster, London SW1

Typeset at Input Typesetting Ltd
and printed in Great Britain by
Richard Clay Ltd, Burgay, Suffolk

# *Contents*

# *Perspective*

At the beginning of 1986 the church which I serve, Harlesden Methodist in north-west London, was gracious enough to give me a three months' sabbatical, after an eleven-year term as minister. I decided to spend it in Nicaragua, a country where Christians were actively participating in a revolutionary struggle to a degree I believed to be unique in modern history. I wanted to learn more at first hand of what was really happening, since I felt western Christians might have much to learn from the Nicaraguan situation. I was not disappointed, and this book is one result of my experience. It is however a book written by a fairly experienced observer, with additional research, rather than an expert, and should be read as such. It is also a book completed at a particular moment in time, the end of 1986, and this too should not be forgotten, as events move with great rapidity in Nicaragua these days.

I should explain at the outset that I write from a political and theological position sympathetic to the Sandinista Revolution. On the other hand I do not wish to be uncritically supportive, either of the Sandinistas or the churches, and I do not believe that I have been. Part of my purpose was to try to learn Spanish, something I have wanted to do for years yet never found the time for. I am grateful for the patience of those Nicaraguan Christians whom I haltingly interviewed in getting my material. I am proud to say that a number of the references in the book are my translations from the original, with a little help from some friends.

I would like to thank those who assisted my pilgrimage, for such I believe it turned out to be: the members of Harlesden Methodist Church, the John Finch trustees, the friends at the Nicaraguan Baptist Convention and Seminary who provided accommodation, guided my studies, arranged interviews and read my draft manuscript; colleagues at CEPAD and CAV who gave time and advice; Kwamla Atteen my Spanish teacher who corrected my translations; Vicky Winston my cheerful and long-suffering secretary who typed out the manuscript – twice; Fr Miguel d'Escoto, the emblem of whose Evangelical Insurrection appears on the cover of this book and other comrades with whom I marched the dusty roads of Nicaragua on the unforgettable *via crucis*. I would also like to thank the CCPD and HRROLA desks of the World Council of Churches, and Christian Aid, for financial support for this publication.

The book is dedicated however to those at the heart of the struggle, the *campesinos* of Nicaragua. It is they who toil, study, build, suffer and keep guard, in order that the Nicaraguan Revolution may survive, and progress. I conclude with the words which one of them, Francisco Aguilera Ruiz, painstakingly wrote in the back of my notebook, when I stayed in his family home during the *via crucis*:

> On the beautiful *via crucis* from Jalapa to Managua we are very pleased to have met David, a Methodist from England. England and Nicaragua are united in Christ the *campesino*, Christ the worker, Christ the poet. We are as people to people like the plants with the sun and the dew. David this is your homeland, Nicaragua, land of lakes and volcanoes, a homeland where there is no religious persecution, a homeland of poets, a homeland of those who struggle for peace and dignified work which is for the benefit of all.

*December 1986*

# Abbreviations

| | |
|---|---|
| ABC | American Baptist Church, USA |
| CAM | Central American Mission |
| CAV | Centro Antonio Valdivieso |
| CBN | Christian Broadcasting Network, USA |
| CEBIC | Consejo Ecumenico de Bluefileñas Iglesias Christianas (Ecumenical Council of Bluefields Christian Churches) |
| CEBs | comunidades eclesiales de base (basic Christian communities) |
| CEPAD | Protestant Committee for Aid to Development |
| CEPRES | Comité Evangelica para Responsibilidad Social (Protestant Committee for Social Responsibility) |
| CIA | Central Intelligence Agency, US Government |
| CLAI | Consejo Latino americano Iglesias (Council of Latin American Churches) |
| CNPEN | Comité Nacional de Pastores Evangelicos de Nicaragua (National Committee for Protestant Pastors of Nicaragua) |
| FDN | Fuerza Democratica Nicaragüense (Nicaraguan Democratic Force) |
| FEET | Facultad Evangélica Estudios Teologicos (The Protestant Institute for Theological Studies) |
| FSLN | Frente Sandinista de Liberación Nacional (Sandinista National Liberation Front) |
| IRD | Institute for Religion and Democracy, USA |
| KISAN | Miskito organization continuing armed resistance to the Sandinistas |

| | |
|---|---|
| NRF | Nicaragua Refugee Fund, USA |
| RIPEN | Retiro Interdenominacional por Pastores Evangelicos de Nicaragua (Interdenominational Retreat of Protestant Pastors of Nicaragua) |
| SMP | Servicio Militar y Patriotica (Patriotic Military Service) |
| USPG | United Society for the Propagation of the Gospel, UK |

# Maps

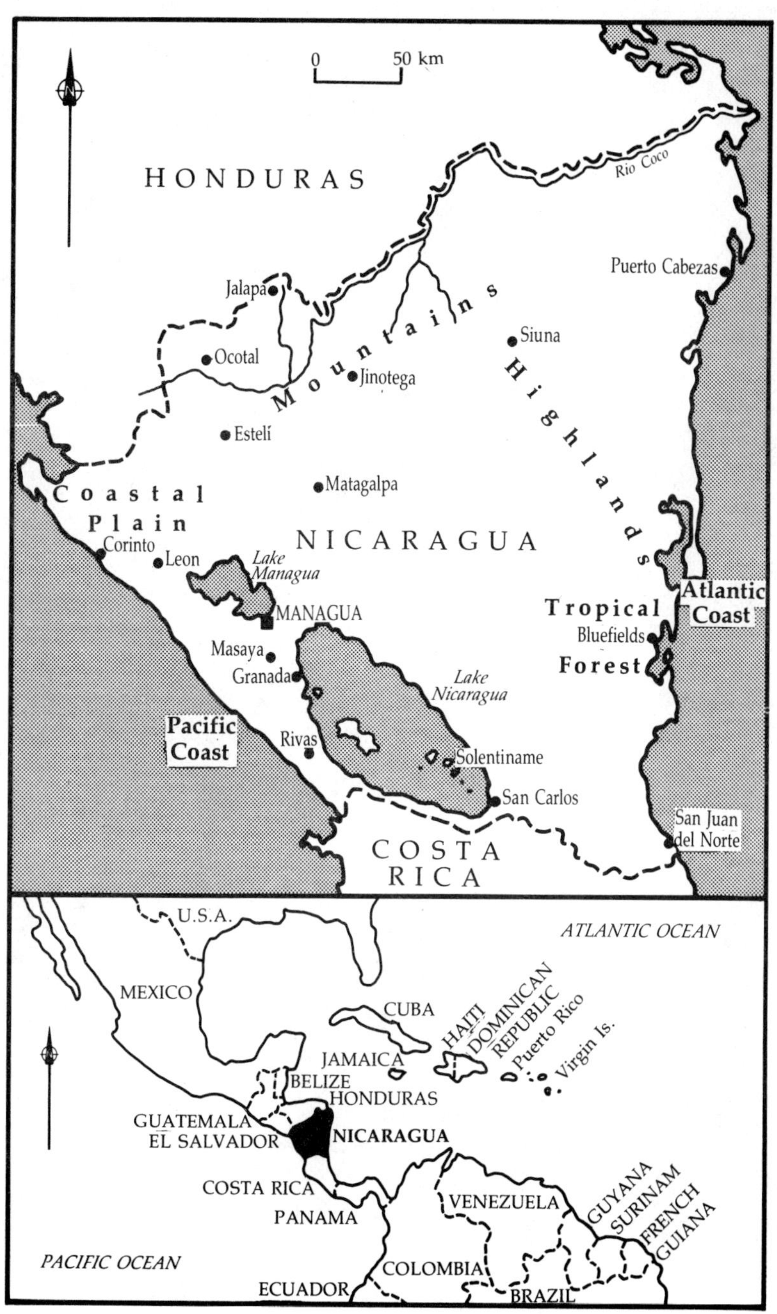

0 50 km
HONDURAS
Rio Coco
Puerto Cabezas
Jalapa
Mountains
Siuna
Ocotal
Jinotega
Highlands
Estelí
Matagalpa
Coastal Plain
NICARAGUA
Corinto
Leon
Lake Managua
Atlantic Coast
Tropical Forest
MANAGUA
Bluefields
Masaya
Granada
Lake Nicaragua
Pacific Coast
Rivas
Solentiname
San Carlos
San Juan del Norte
COSTA RICA
U.S.A.
ATLANTIC OCEAN
MEXICO
CUBA
HAITI
DOMINICAN REPUBLIC
Puerto Rico
Virgin Is.
JAMAICA
BELIZE
HONDURAS
GUATEMALA
EL SALVADOR
NICARAGUA
COSTA RICA
VENEZUELA
GUYANA
SURINAM
FRENCH GUIANA
PANAMA
PACIFIC OCEAN
COLOMBIA
ECUADOR
BRAZIL

# 1

# *Conquistadores* and Missionaries – The Evolution of Nation and Church

## *Colonialism and its Consequences*

The original inhabitants of Central America were Indian peoples whose descendants today still occupy parts of Guatemala, Honduras, Nicaragua and Panama, despite the depredations over the centuries of Spanish, English and North American colonists. They were present when Columbus 'discovered' the Americas at the end of the fifteenth century, and some of them were the ancestors of the Miskito, Sumu and Rama people who now live in the eastern region of Nicaragua. Following the exploratory journeys of Columbus and others, the Spanish began to colonize the Pacific coasts of South America, eventually finding their way northwards to Nicaragua. As was their custom they conquered the land unceremoniously, treating with brutality any opposition by the native peoples. Meanwhile the English in the sixteenth and seventeenth centuries gained the ascendancy in the Caribbean, and duly extended this to the Atlantic (eastern) coast of Central America.

The English presence in the sixteenth century on the Atlantic coast consisted mainly of buccaneers such as Drake, Hawkins and Morgan. They made their first base the area which is now the country of Belize, but in the early seventeenth century they spread southwards into the east coastal region of Nicaragua. The buccaneers brought in farming interests and assisted in the setting up of the Providence Company, which became the main channel through which the Atlantic coast and its people were milked of their resources such as indigo and wood. Sugar plantations were also introduced. By force and persuasion they adopted the local inhabitants, who later came to be called 'Miskitos' (some say this was derived from the great number of mosquitoes present, others to the muskets the English gave them). The English then used them in the war against the Spanish, repelling Spanish efforts to take over the eastern region. The English also brought in African slaves from the Caribbean to work the plantations; these English-speaking blacks came to be known as Creoles.

Britain remained the sole power on the Atlantic coast until 1850 when the United States began to look for domination over the southern half of the American continent. At the same time plans were being made for the construction of a canal across the Central American isthmus, and one suggested route was via the two large lakes in southern Nicaragua. Along with US geo-political interest came commercial enterprises such as the United Fruit Company; it and others proceeded vigorously to exploit agricultural resources such as banana and mahogany, and to mine the gold found some seventy miles inland. The profit from all such resources found its way to the United States and Europe. This foreign economic exploitation has remained a dominant factor in the area ever since. Meanwhile on the Pacific coast the struggle for independence from Spain had been won. The Central American region became independent from 1821 and Nicaragua became a separate republic in 1838. The Pacific west was however quite unable to exert any influence over the eastern half of the country and this separation of geography, history, culture (including language), economy and political control has been another major factor in the form of Nicaragua's development up to the present time.

The main result in religious terms of the Spanish domination of the west coast was the accompanying influence of the Catholic church. Wherever the main towns grew up, automatically dominating the central square was the large Catholic church or cathedral. The church existed mostly in close relationship with the political and military power, and bishops tended to change fairly rapidly, not always under instructions from the mother church in Spain. Occasionally a bishop arose such as Antonio Valdivieso, in the sixteenth century, who sought to protect the rights of the indigenous people against the depredations of the military, but it was not long before he was martyred. Catholicism existed mostly as a means of meeting the formal religious needs of baptism, regular communion, marriage and burial of the Spanish population and, where indigenous people survived, of incorporating them into the political and religious system. The historical dominance of the Catholic church on the Pacific coast is a further important dimension of the context in which the Protestant churches later made their arrival in Nicaragua.

The nineteenth century witnessed the gradual evolution of conflict between the two sections of the oligarchy, the 'conservatives' (who were in fact strongly allied with the Catholic church) and the 'liberals' (perhaps slightly more conscious of the needs of the less privileged). It also saw the growing interest of the United States in power in the region, including the extraordinary episode of the ambitious mercenary William Walker who took over the country for a time, and the attempts from the Pacific side to unify the country by imposing some control over the Atlantic coast. A degree of stability was achieved under the nationalist Liberal government of General José Santos Zelaya at the end of the nineteenth century, who among other things guaranteed freedom of worship for all, took away some of the Catholic church's lands and introduced civil marriage and divorce. Eventually however Zelaya's nationalism was too much for the United States, which in its first direct intervention linked up with the Conservative party to overthrow him in 1909. The subsequent period of US domination was opposed by popular uprisings and also by Bishop Pereira y Castellón, who has been called the first anti-imperialist bishop for his letter to the North American Cardinal Simpson in 1912, protesting against US interference. The US-Nicaragua treaty signed at that time, giving the United States rights to build and control an inter-oceanic canal, was another symbol of the drive to North American hegemony – it did not actually wish to build a canal, merely to prevent anyone else from doing so and thereby competing with the one in Panama.

In 1926 Nicaraguan nationalism erupted in a new form, this time under the leadership of the famous general Augusto C. Sandino, who with his small army of *campesinos* fought the US occupation until the North Americans were finally forced to withdraw in 1932. In describing Sandino's army, as in all cases when referring to the poorer rural population, the Spanish term *campesino* is used, which has now correctly been invested with much more dignity and worth than the direct English translation 'peasant'. In Sandino is found the fascinating mixture of nationalism, socialism and Christianity which has been present in all the Nicaraguan independence struggles this century. 'Sandino was profoundly religious, Christian, although not a part of institutional Christianity. He believed his cause was invincible because God was with his struggle. Jesus was for him one who struggled for justice and freedom, and all who struggle for the people's liberation are bearers of his teaching. Sandino taught these things to his army.'[1]

The US then changed its strategy, encouraging the installation of a régime of the liberal tradition, eventually led by Anastasio Somoza, and training a National Guard to ensure that the régime would last. The first Somoza crowned his allegiance to his North American masters by having Sandino assassinated immediately following a peace conference in 1934. Hence the new model of US imperialism was established: the military dictatorship. Anastasio was himself shot by a young poet-follower of Sandino in 1956, when he was succeeded first by his elder then his younger son, the latter also named Anastasio. During this period the Sandinista movement struggled on weakly, with the successful assassination of Anastasio Somoza but also some failed uprisings.

It was some twenty-five years before the spirit of Sandino again seriously affected the Nicaraguan people, with the formation of the Frente Sandinista de Liberación Nacional (FSLN) in 1961. The first years were hard and the FSLN suffered, particularly in 1967. Somoza was enormously rich and powerful and his National Guard had full access to US military support and equipment. However, during the 1970s the reinvigorated FSLN began to succeed in winning over many of the *campesinos*, the urban workers, the youth and the students. They were assisted by the Somoza clique's own arrogance and brutality towards any critic who dared to surface, and its blatant corruption following the international response to the 1972 earthquake. In their ideology the Sandinistas retained Sandino's mixture of nationalism, socialism and Christianity. They became increasingly effective militarily and in late 1977 they called for a united front in opposition to Somoza. The turbulence spread through the whole country, culminating in the unsuccessful insurrection of August-September 1978 in which the National Guard used artillery and aerial bombing on Nicaragua's cities and 5,000 people were killed. Somoza's continued refusal to negotiate even with the political centre, despite US pressure, led to his complete isolation by the middle of 1979 when the final Sandinista-led insurrection began. By mid-July Somoza had fled, leaving the FSLN in control, much to the chagrin of the United States government which had hoped to see a centrist alliance deny full power to the Sandinistas. Almost from that point the US began to try to destabilize the new Nicaraguan government, having sought unsuccessfully to exclude those who had borne the chief burden of the struggle from the fruits of all their efforts.

It is vital in this historical outline to understand the nature of the North American perspective. The United States bases its view of Latin America on the so-called Monroe doctrine, named after the US president who in 1823 announced to the rest of the world that the whole of the American continent was to be regarded as a field of US interests, and other nations would not be permitted more than a passing glance or a modest investment. The interlocking of economic and religious interests as a result of this is reflected in a fascinating letter dated 1905 by a US Baptist missionary F. T. Gates who said, among other things, 'The imports from pagan lands provide us with many luxuries of life at low price, no few commodities, and many things which we now consider necessities . . . our imports are balanced by our exports to these same countries . . . such growth would have been impossible without the commercial conquest of foreign lands under the initiative of missionary forces.'[2] The decades that followed were to see increasing US control over Latin America.

In more recent years the Rockefeller mission to South America in 1969, which occasioned opposition and rioting in a number of countries, was intended both to reassert US hegemony and also to uncover dissent to North American imperialism. The Rockefeller report included reference to the church, when it commented on the need to observe carefully the development of the 'theology of liberation', and suggested that judicious support for some of the Protestant churches might be a way of undermining a Catholic church which, following the progressive conclusions of the Latin American bishops' conference at Medellín in 1968, seemed to be moving forward as hoped for by the liberation theologians. The thinking which guides the current US administration is encapsulated in the so-called Santa Fe Report, produced in 1980 by a conservative 'think-tank', the Council for Inter-American Security. It points out the crucial importance of the Latin American subcontinent for the USA: 7,000 miles long, 16% of the world's land-mass and 10% of its people. If the US fails to remain in economic control of the region, it says, 'we are by omission encouraging our southern neighbours to embrace the Soviet bear'.[3] It is this kind of thinking which enables the USA to fund the counter-revolutionary, or *contra*, activity which has caused such controversy both in the United States and in Europe. In the section on 'Internal Subversion' on the continent the document states:

> US foreign policy must begin to counter (not react against) liberation theology as it is utilised in Latin America by 'liberation theology clergy'. The role of the church in Latin America is vital to the concept of political freedom. Unfortunately Marxist-Leninist forces have utilised the church as a political weapon against private property and productive capitalism by infiltrating the religious community with ideas that are less Christian than Communist.[4]

Hence religion is seen by those most committed to US expansionism as part of the battle-ground for the hearts and minds, as well as the labour and resources, of the nations of Latin America.

These then are the main dimensions of the context in which we must see the arrival of, the growth of and the current struggles within the Protestant churches in Nicaragua. The historical divisions of geography, history, culture and economy between the eastern and western halves of the country, the dominance of Catholicism on the Pacific coast, the rising desire over 150 years by an increasingly imperialistic United States for political and economic domination, and the mixture of nationalism, socialism and Christianity which for over a century has fuelled the resulting struggle for a free Nicaragua. These are some of the consequences of colonialism in Central America.

## *The Advent of the Protestant Churches*

There is a somewhat romantic notion that the first Protestants to arrive in Nicaragua were the privateers such as Hawkins and Drake who were officially Anglicans and even carried chaplains on some of their boats. In *El Protestantismo en Centro América* Wilton M. Nelson writes,

> It is curious to note how they gave a religious appearance to their activities. Says the Anglican priest of Belize, Stephen Caiger, 'They conceived the sacking of Spanish galleons as a holy war against the greed of the Spanish and the cruelty of the Inquisition.' Each boat had a Bible on which the pirates placed their hand to swear fidelity to 'the brotherhood'.[5]

This suggestion as to its origins is however rather wistfully rejected by the present Anglican church in Nicaragua. Nevertheless, thanks to the effective record-keeping of the Spanish Inquisition, we do know that Protestants have existed in the region for over 400 years. There were in Central America in the sixteenth century 'a total of twenty-one denunciations and reports of signs of Protestantism'.[6] In this section we shall review the development of Protestantism from its beginnings to the coming of the revolution in 1979.

It is perhaps important at this point to comment on the use of the terms 'Protestant' and 'Evangelical'. The latter is much more common in Latin America; for example, groupings of Protestant churches are referred to as 'Evangelical Councils of Churches'. However in European and North American usage 'evangelical' refers to a particular form of Christian belief and practice, often comprising a conservative approach to biblical teaching, an emphasis on individual conversion and a very limited interest in social and economic matters. This is not true of many 'evangelical' churches in Latin America; we shall therefore normally use the term 'Protestant' to refer to all non-Roman Catholic denominations, though 'evangelical' is also occasionally used to describe a more conservative theological approach.

The initial reason for the coming of the Protestants to Central America – apart from as pirates – was the invitation in the mid-nineteenth century to Europeans to emigrate in order to assist the new republics in their economic progress. Observers of the time noted that it would be necessary, in order to attract such immigrants, to guarantee freedom of non-Catholic worship and belief, which duly became Central American law in 1835. This was just in time to benefit from the political upheavals of the 1840s in western Europe, and some British and Germans soon arrived, partly it seems to escape political persecution. The first Protestant church in the region – an Anglican one – had been erected in Belize in 1815, and in 1848 an English sea-captain in Nicaragua's southern neighbour, Costa Rica, obtained official permission for Protestant worship: a church was erected there in 1865.

In Nicaragua itself, the first Anglican settlers on the east coast had made some early contacts with the Miskito, but it was in fact the Moravian church which initiated the first serious Protestant missionary work, largely due to its active presence not far away in Jamaica. We therefore look first at the Moravians, then the Baptists and Anglicans, and finally at two of the fundamentalist-style churches, the Central American Mission and the Assemblies of God. Here we shall deal simply with their historical development, discussion of their theological and political role comes later.

It was with the encouragement of the English, still then controlling the eastern Atlantic coast, that a small exploratory mission arrived from the Moravian community of Herrnhut in 1847, travelling with the assistance of Moravians already in Jamaica. After some months the group returned to Germany and there in 1848 the Moravians decided they would begin their work in Bluefields, in the south of the coastal area, the following year. In Bishop John Wilson's study *El Trabajo Morava en Nicaragua*[7] he describes five stages of expansion of the work between 1849 and 1974, including a revival between 1881 and 1896 when an evangelical and almost pentecostal form of Moravianism spread throughout much of the coastal region.

Wilson goes on to describe the various areas of Moravian activity, including education, health, literacy, and theological development. The Moravians built schools in Bluefields (1921), Puerto Cabezas (1954) and Pearl Lagoon. They constructed the first hospital in the eastern region at Bilwaskama in 1936, took over the Seventh Day Adventist hospital at Puerto Cabezas in 1958 and opened several clinics and a school of nursing. They produced the first Miskito dictionary, a Miskito hymn book in 1893, the New Testament in 1905 and selections from the Old Testament in 1915. In 1969 they began a joint work with the Catholics on a new version of the New Testament in Miskito which was published in 1974; the Old Testament is currently near to completion. These biblical projects are typical of the Moravians' ecumenical approach. Moravian missionaries began pastoral training in theological summer schools in 1925 and later started a theological college. The church was a keen participant in the evangelical campaigns which began on the Atlantic coast in 1951. From the ecumenical contacts built up from these there came a spirit of ecumenism not common in Nicaragua which led to a progressive evangelical campaign in 1967, in which Baptist and Anglican churches, the Church of God and the Assemblies of God were included, as well as the Moravians.

According to Norman Bent, pastor of the Moravian community in the Nicaraguan capital, Managua, it was in about 1963 that the first questionings of missionary control began to disturb the minds of Nicaraguan Moravians.[8] Some of the younger candidate pastors who had gone to Costa Rica for training returned and began to coordinate a programme of consciousness-raising for the people, including week-long seminars for pastors and lay leaders. In 1972 this gave birth to ALPROMISU, a Miskito-Sumu organization begun by Moravian pastor Wycliffe Diego. Somoza dubbed this whole process a Communist movement. These pastors also began to press for more independence from the mother church. By 1970 this was being promised for the end of the decade but in 1974 the missionaries summarily announced the church's autonomy and by the end of that year all had left. It took the young and inexperienced new leadership some little time to adjust to the new situation. The indigenous peoples have continued to be keen adherents of the church; many of its pastors are Miskito.

The Moravians, being mainly confined to the Atlantic coast, saw very little of the revolutionary struggle. In fact many east-coast Nicaraguans had not really heard of the Sandinistas until 1979, when Somoza was overthrown, much less understood what they stood for. A Baptist minister serving in Puerto Cabezas for the last twenty years commented, 'We knew of two brothers imprisoned, so it was said, for being "Communists", but because Somoza prevented any politicization, few people even knew of the Sandinista movement.'[9] A Moravian remarked that it was only when it was discovered that people could listen to Radio Sandino in late 1978 that much became known about the Pacific coast. This partly explains some of the later difficulties on the eastern side of the country when the Sandinistas tried to establish themselves. The main concern for the Miskitos – and therefore for the Moravians – was the independence of their own communities. Having achieved a certain degree of independence, and having felt far less oppressed by Somoza than people in the west, the Moravian membership was more than a little suspicious as to the motivation of the new revolution.

Alongside the Moravians the Methodists made a small contribution in the mid-nineteenth century. There is mention of a Methodist missionary in the 1830s in the Bluefields area for some eighteen months, during which time he taught local people to read the Bible. Again in the 1950s Methodists from Panama participated along with Moravians in evangelical campaigns on the east coast, and in 1986 there were six United Methodist (USA) missionaries in Nicaragua, providing an information service and the infrastructure for educational visits, and working in forestry and speech therapy.

It was the Baptists however who were next to develop enduring work on the east coast. The first Baptist presence was on Corn

Island, one of two inhabited islands some forty miles off Bluefields, in the Caribbean Sea. In 1852 Rev. Edward Kelly arrived from Belize and began the Ebenezer Baptist Church. Small churches were also developed later in Bluefields and Puerto Cabezas, which still survive. Zion Baptist in Bluefields, which has its own junior school, was opened in 1922. It was not until 1932 however that the Atlantic coast Baptists were 'discovered' by those from the Pacific side of the country.

The beginnings of the Baptist work on the west coast are slightly confused, depending upon who is regarded as a Baptist missionary. There was certainly sufficient Baptist presence for the American Baptist Missionary Society, based in New York, to commence work in Nicaragua in 1917, the date from which the formation of the Nicaraguan Baptist Church is now usually measured.[10] Some activity had begun earlier when Eleanor Blackmore, an English missionary originally with the Central American Mission, broke away in 1911 and linked up with other Baptists already present. Not long after this came the Panama Conference of 1916, when representatives of the North American churches met and 'parcelled out' the countries of Central America, deciding which should be the mission field of each denomination.

Miss Blackmore was then appointed a missionary of the Women's Society of the American Baptist Church. She teamed up with Rev. José Mendoza and together they opened the First Baptist Church of Managua in 1917. The missionaries built up congregations in various towns including Masaya and León in the next three years, although the Baptists were plagued at an early stage by a common feature of Protestant life in Nicaragua when the Managua church split and Rev. José Mendoza set up the First Evangelical Independent Baptist Church in Managua. Work evolved in Rivas and Masatepe and by 1930 the Managua Baptists had opened schools and a hospital. Having made connections with the Atlantic Baptists, in 1937 the Baptists were able to form the Baptist Convention of Nicaragua. The social dimension of the Baptist work was concentrated in Managua, where by 1942 the First Baptist Church had increased to 624 members, with 800 pupils in the Bible school. One reason for this growth was the development of the Baptist high school and hospital, both much needed in an environment where Catholic control of social agencies made life very difficult for Protestants. It is worth noting that the first director, doctor and principal nurse of the hospital were all women, as were most of those who earlier brought the Baptist high school into being. The health work led to the setting up of Provadenic, which is still the key church health agency committed to the rural sector in Nicaragua today. The Baptists began their theological seminary in 1941 in Masaya, though it has now moved to Managua, on a joint site with the Convention headquarters.

The focus on education and theological training paid off and may have been one of the factors in the way in which the Baptist church was somewhat better prepared for the events of 1979 than the other Protestant churches. The dean of the Baptist Seminary, Jerjez Ruiz, in a paper written with US Baptist Douglass Sullivan, comments that this lack of readiness may partly have been because Nicaraguan Christians – at least the majority – seem to have looked to the continent of South America, specifically the southern cone, for the new prophetic conscience and action.[11] Ruiz goes on to point out however that there was a group of young Baptists – Julio López, Lea Guido and José Miguel Torres, who sought to respond actively to the theology of Dietrich Bonhoeffer, Martin Luther King and Emilio Castro (now General Secretary of the World Council of Churches). During the late 1960s and early 1970s these and other young leaders caused much disturbance in the Baptist churches, initiating discussions on North American imperialism and the possibilities of socialism. 'The basic historical context of that movement,' says Ruiz, 'was the existence of the guerrilla struggle of the FSLN, the international event of the Cuban Revolution, the existence of the Alliance for Progress and the repression of the Somoza dictatorship.' (The Alliance is the US-dominated political forum for the American continent.)

During this period the Baptists also became more independent of US missionary influence, though they had perhaps been fortunate in being linked with the American Baptist church, who were more relaxed about such changes than the more conservative Southern

Baptists. They achieved formal autonomy in 1974. Hence the Baptist Convention was relatively well-placed to make a positive response to the Sandinista Revolution when it came.

In terms of historical development we next turn to the Anglicans, or the Episcopal church as it is now known in Nicaragua. Anglicans decline to locate their arrival in the country with the presence of the buccaneers, but according to the records of the USPG (United Society for the Propagation of the Gospel) as early as 1742 a Mr Hodgson was sent to the indigenous people of the Atlantic coast, along with thirty soldiers. He had 'some success with civilizing the Miskitos' and also in carrying out 'the immediate intention of heading the Indians against the Spaniards with whom the British were at war',[12] apparently an essential part of his missionary activity. Another lay man Christian Frederick Post offered a ministry in the area for several decades till he died in 1785. After Post's death the Miskitos ministered to themselves for over 100 years. In the middle of the eighteenth century an Anglican priest, Rev. Nathan Price, who was reported to have some connections both with the buccaneers and the USPG, said an occasional mass at Greytown, in the far south of Nicaragua's east coast, and there is evidence that two travellers came across an English Protestant Church there in the mid-nineteenth century.[13] It is unclear whether this served Miskitos or the English-speaking community. The formal position of the Anglicans is that the church established itself in the nineteenth century in the Greytown area, due to plantation-owners moving across from Jamaica and other Caribbean islands. Later it moved to Bluefields and the work at Greytown collapsed. St. Mark's Church, Bluefields was opened in 1898. Educational work was also begun, and St. Mark's College continues today as an Anglican school.

As a result of this Anglican renewal a re-connection was made with the Miskitos to the north, who soon asked for a priest to come and baptize some 125 people in the Pearl Lagoon area. The tradition of lay ministry there continued strong. Especially remembered is David 'Daddy' Green who in the second decade of this century established permanent programmes of worship among Creoles and

Miskitos in the Pearl Lagoon area.[14] The work spread north, to Puerto Cabezas, and also out to Corn Island.

The church developed in traditional Anglican terms. 'St. Mark's Church, Bluefields, was very much like a British parish church located in Nicaraguan jungle. The church members, although Nicaraguan, saw themselves as British.'[15] Eventually however declining British involvement on the Atlantic coast and increasing US strategic interests resulted in 1942 in a hand-over of the responsibility for the Nicaraguan Anglicans to the Episcopal Church of the USA. This led to a rather different emphasis, and in 1951 the first Anglican church on the Pacific side of the country was opened, near Managua, though for its first four years it was ministered to by the priest from Bluefields. Although the first Nicaraguan was ordained in 1965, the Anglicans seem not to have seen themselves as an indigenous church. Because of its earlier dependence on the Anglican churches of both England and the United States 'the Episcopal church of Nicaragua has deprived itself of Nicaraguan and Latin American dialogue and theological reflection, and of broadening its relationships with the Protestant and Catholic churches of the Pacific'.[16] The bishop remained a US citizen, appointed from North America. This symbolized the ambivalence of the missionary relationship. 'American missionaries, as the British before them, brought much to the Nicaraguan church. They also, however, had a tendency to dominate the church. They offered more than a presence. They brought to the church an American ethos and way of doing things. Helpful as some of this may have been it was not Nicaraguan.'[17] Such was the power of the missionary ideology, leading to a church which, until very recently, has been a foreign rather than a local institution.

This led to a situation where the church was not really ready for the events of 1979. 'The Episcopal church was not prepared for the revolution. There was anger on the part of some Episcopalians that the church had not better prepared them. In various ways the Episcopal church, along with most of the other churches, was identified with the Somoza régime.'[18] Hence, as for many Protestant

Christians, the events of 1979 came as a shock to those sheltered in the life of the Nicaraguan Episcopalian church.

One of the first of the more fundamentalist churches, as it would be described in British terms, to begin work in Nicaragua was the Central American Mission (CAM), initiated by Cyrus Scofield of Dallas, Texas. The CAM might almost be described as a sect; such definitions are discussed further in chapter five. It bases itself upon the *Scofield Reference Bible*, a rather peculiar work edited by Dr Scofield, which claimed to show that the Bible predicted seven specific ages of humanity. The CAM's first missionary in Nicaragua was Alfredo Roos, who arrived in 1900 from Costa Rica with his wife, at the age of twenty-four. He was joined in 1903 by Eleanor Blackmore, who later transferred to Baptist work, but between them they started churches, prepared preachers, opened a hostel for orphans and did other social work. Roos continued his work until 1912, and laid the foundation for the continuing presence of the CAM in Nicaragua.

Another important fundamentalist type of church in the country is the Assemblies of God, which dates its beginning from the arrival of a North American pentecostal preacher Venus Shoenckey in 1912. He started work in León and Matagalpa in 1915, and moved on to Estelí.[19] The Assemblies still only reported fifty members in the early 1930s, with one church and two preaching places,[20] but around this time new missionaries arrived from the US and in 1936 it declared itself independent from the mother convention, although it retained strong ties. An interesting anecdote from this time recalls that, under some harassment from the Catholic church in the northern Matagalpa area, the Assemblies' members appealed to General Sandino, who gave them one of his flags to serve as protection against hostile Catholics.[21] The church grew steadily and in 1958 extended itself by evangelical campaigns on the east coast, establishing congregations in Bluefields, Corn Island, Puerto Cabezas and along the Rio Coco on Nicaragua's northern border. We shall examine the Assemblies in more detail in the next chapter, and their response to the coming of the revolution.

The mid-period of the twentieth century had two main characteristics as far as the development of Protestantism was concerned; a period of consolidation of the main denominations and the beginning of the 'denominational explosion' which rapidly increased the numbers of churches in the country. With respect to consolidation, the Assemblies of God tended to concentrate themselves in the Matagalpa region in the north, the CAM round Rivas and Granada in the south, the Baptists in Managua and the Moravians and Anglicans on the east coast. This period included the development of social work such as schools and hospitals. In the 1940s however the explosion began, commencing with the arrival of the Church of God, the Church of God of Prophecy, the Mennonites, the International Baptist Church (linked to an independent Baptist Church in Chattanooga, Tennessee), the Apostolic Church of the Faith in Jesus Christ (now one of the largest denominations), the Free Apostolic Church and the United Evangelical Pentecostal Mission. All these reported at least 2,000 members by the time the first survey of the churches was conducted by CEPAD, with a regional research institute, in 1980.[22] The period between 1940 and 1970 has also been referred to as a 'sheep-stealing' period, where there was vigorous competition between the churches for members, manifesting divisiveness, denominational imperialism and territorialism. The deep suspicions between denominations persisted into the 1970s, but it might be said that in 1972 the Nicaraguan earthquake brought the churches to their senses.

There are some very critical views of the role of the Protestant churches in the pre-revolutionary period. One of the young Baptist pastors referred to above, José Miguel Torres, made a presentation at a five-day seminar held in Managua in September 1979, just three months after the revolutionary triumph, outlining the difficulties under which radical Christians had been operating. They had

> a Protestant church coming out of the USA which appeared like a missionary project on the stage of the imperialist expansion of the capitalist system, a church which in the preceding period reproduced the life-model of the North American missionary . . . a church which by its puritan, pietistic nature fell into a position

> of neutrality . . . in more modern parlance, a social democratic church. It was a missionary project, so that while imperialistic capital strengthened its relationship with the dominant sectors . . . of our Nicaraguan society, this project launched itself at the lower classes of society. It identified . . . with the liberal ideology of 'live and let live'; but in a class-divided society it made the church into a legitimation of the liberal government's inability to accept the possibility of social change which would be outside the capitalist system.[23]

Torres went on to claim that those who sought to form a new radical church, which declared for the 'class option' were often 'expelled from the churches, erased from the Book of the Baptized, denied recognition, disparaged . . .', though others contest this view.

It would not be correct to leave this section without referring to the work of the Bible Societies in Nicaragua. The first American Bible Society colporteur to arrive was Rev. Wheeler in 1856. Unfortunately for him he arrived at about the time that his countryman, William Walker (who was mentioned earlier) sought to take over the country. The 'Nicaraguan enemies of Walker demanded that Wheeler join them in order to fight the filibusterers. For his refusal he was shot at the end of 1856 and thus ended the first effort to establish a Bible Society in Nicaragua'.[24] More successful was the venture of Francisco Penzotti, representing both the US and British and Foreign Bible Societies, who arrived at the end of the century. He laid the foundation, amidst Catholic opposition, for the Nicaraguan Bible Society which much later made such a contribution to the Literacy Crusade after the revolution.

We have referred briefly on one or two occasions to the hostility of the Catholic church to the coming of the Protestants. This factor is important to note for its effect on ecumenical relationships right up to the present day. It appears to have begun during the Inquisition of the seventeenth century, and the accusations against Protestants even into the current century included refusal to venerate the Virgin, distributing a mutilated and unauthorized Bible, preaching justification by faith alone and rejection of papal authority. In addition

Protestant growth was regarded as harmful socially and politically to Central America as a whole, where it was felt to threaten local unity. In the last hundred years Protestantism has been successively accused by conservative Catholics of bringing British domination, North American domination, and Communist domination.[25] Even until fifteen years ago Protestants were harassed in their schooling or their employment, Catholics climbed on chapel roofs during services, threw rocks at people coming to worship and occasionally burned chapels or pastors' homes. In the Baptist chapel of San Gregoria, in the Nuevo Segovia district, there is a cross at the place where elderly Feliciano Cerrato was cut to death by the machetes of enraged Catholics in 1963. A number of Protestant pastors have stories from the late 1960s of being stoned while going to preach. It should be said this mostly took place in the Catholic stronghold of the Pacific coastal region; attitudes in the east seem to have been much calmer. The anti-ecumenical atmosphere began to change after the Second Vatican Council.

A further point worth noting is that the Protestant missionaries operated initially almost entirely among the poor. This was partly because at least to some degree the Catholic church had abandoned the underprivileged, and hence they had little to lose by espousing Protestantism. The little evangelical group also gave them some importance, where they might be lost in the great amorphous mass of Catholicism. 'A person was taken account of, given something to do, sang hymns in worship, there were joyful choirs, people gave testimonies and sometimes received material help.'[26] The social elements which supported the Liberal parties favoured the Protestants for breaking the religious hegemony of the Catholic church, but few actually joined for fear of the stigma attached. It should also be said that some of the Protestants were fairly aggressive in their anti-Catholicism, criticizing the images and relics, the worshipping of the saints, Mariolatry and the ostentation of worship, and this did not help ecumenical relations. Their own worship was Bible-based and simple, their beliefs emphasized personal conversion and justification by faith, and they demanded strict standards of behaviour from their members – no smoking, drinking, dancing, theatre, cinema, marital infidelity or – more recently – cosmetics or hairstyling for women. Many of these characteristics of early Protestantism remain in evidence today.

The Protestant churches, although they ministered among the poor, did not really seek to assist them in identifying the causes of their problems, nor to demand solutions, especially as the problems intensified under the Somoza régime. Robert Renouf, describing in particular the Atlantic coast, sums it up admirably:

> A legacy of oppression was deeply rooted in the lives of the people. Despite the poverty and neglect by Somoza and the foreign corporations many, if not the majority, of the coastal people saw the period of Somoza's 'hands-off policy' and foreign domination as positive and regarded it as 'the good old days' when they were taken care of by the government and churches. The churches, Anglican, Moravian and Roman Catholic, did not speak out against the oppression by Somoza and the foreign interests.[27]

One final factor which needs to be mentioned before leaving our historical glance at the motivations and effects of the missionary initiative is the prevalent North American influence in the growth of Protestantism in Nicaragua, particularly during this century. The pervasiveness of US involvement in all parts of Latin American life has been referred to earlier and it is certainly true in the sphere of the Protestant churches. Almost all the major denominations in Nicaragua have had direct US assistance – and therefore at least some control – including the CAM, the Assemblies of God, the Baptists and Anglican/Episcopalians, and even the Moravians, with their links with the Moravian Board of Foreign Missions in Bethlehem, Philadelphia.

In particular among the more evangelical and pentecostal churches, many of which have arisen in the last thirty years, the stimulation and material support in order to start up have often stemmed from the USA. It is also important to recognize the conservative nature of many of the US missionary bodies and their personnel, from both the mainstream and the fundamentalist Protestant churches. Along with a conservative theology has usually come an anti-Communism which was a product of social and political thinking in the United States during the first half of the twentieth century. Hence those who have begun to make social or political comment out of their biblical studies, or latterly to explore the theology of liberation, have been regarded as deeply suspect by some Protestants. For Nicaraguan Protestants this became more and more sharply defined in the Somoza era, not least because the prevalent pro-North Americanism bestowed on anything coming out of the USA something akin to divine status. For Somoza this whole process was all to the good. It helped to keep the people occupied and satisfactorily turned their minds from any thought of social change. The plethora of churches or sects which arrived in the 1960s and 1970s, and their capacity for schism, also meant a fragmentation of the people, which clearly benefitted the dictatorship. Recalling the comments of the Rockefeller Report of 1969, it is hard not to conclude that, whether or not the Holy Spirit was a partner in these missionary enterprises, the US intelligence services were not at all unhappy as they observed the general trend.

*Conquistadores* and missionaries therefore both played their part in creating the economic, political and social conditions which pertained in Nicaragua in the 1970s. With their determination to imprint their secular and religious dominance on both the indigenous people of the country and those brought from Africa or Europe to supply the labour, these two groups helped to create the soil in which the Sandinista Revolution took root. It may be said with some truth that the faith which at least some of the missionaries provided helped to initiate and sustain the most positive dimensions of the struggle for change. It may also be said that some forms of Christianity laid upon the Nicaraguan people were much more about sedation than inspiration, about control than liberation. Let us however examine the evolution of the Protestant churches since 1979, and the current issues facing them in the social and political upheavals taking place in the new Nicaragua.

# 2

# Challenge and Change – The Protestant Churches Since the Revolution

Before going on to examine the way in which the churches have reacted to the events of 1979, it is important to have at least a basic understanding of the pressures which led up to the revolution, and the response of Christians and churches to them.

The Sandinista National Liberation Front (FSLN), the vanguard of the opposition to the Somoza dictatorship, had been formed in 1961. After initial struggles to establish itself, it came under strong pressure in the late 1960s and survived only by the determination of a few. When one of the most traumatic events in Nicaragua's history took place, the earthquake of 1972, the FSLN was beginning to re-establish itself in the north. It was the mis-handling of the generous and widespread aid received for the earthquake that began to convince many in Nicaragua, including church leaders, that Somoza was beyond redemption – at least in this life – and that he would have to go. Millions of pounds donated for earthquake relief either disappeared, were used to purchase inappropriate assistance, or were channelled into companies controlled by Somoza as payments for the work of reconstruction – very little of which was then carried out. In addition the distribution of land and wealth was becoming more and more unjust, and housing, education and health services were either standing still or deteriorating. Furthermore, the régime behaved quite viciously towards any who organized in opposition to it.

As protests built up, both Catholics and Protestants began to grow increasingly concerned and angry. Some Catholics in the basic Christian communities (CEBs) began to organize specifically against the régime, believing that it had become so tyrannical that it was a Christian duty actively to oppose it. Some Catholics joined the FSLN, and many of the base communities became supportive of the movement for national liberation.

There is a thesis that the Nicaraguan Revolution would not have been possible without the CEBs. This was because of the communication network they began to provide for the underground Sandinista forces, in terms of messages, food, safe houses, transport and arms storage. This was particularly the case in 1978/9, when the struggle reached its height and the co-operation of a wide range of groups and individuals throughout the western half of the country was essential. Whether or not this thesis is true, it has to be said that there were very few such Protestant groups involved in laying the foundations for the successful insurrection of 1979, though there were individual Protestants who actively participated.

Furthermore, the achievements of 1979 should be seen in the context of the brutality of the US-trained National Guard, which increased considerably during the late 1970s, as it found itself under attack from all directions and throughout the western half of the country. It should also be remembered that the dictator Somoza, in the final weeks of his power, was sending the heavily-armed Guard into local communities where the people fought back with barricades, sticks and stones and any bits of armaments they had been able to capture. They had a fierce determination to resist. Somoza's air force also attacked great areas of Nicaragua's towns and cities, including Managua, León and Estelí, reducing to rubble parts of some *barrios* (as urban communities are usually known in Latin America). Christians, like everyone else, were forced to choose which side they were on, and at that point many Protestants bravely joined the insurrection. On the whole however Protestants appear to have been denied the kind of theological, historical and political analysis which went on in and around the CEBs and provided the perspective for their radical activities. It is of course the remnants of the National

Guard who continue to provide the core of the infamous *contras*, with their brutal raids into Nicaragua from neighbouring Honduras.

Let us now explore the response of the Protestant churches to the revolutionary situation and see what is to be learned, examine what kind of faith existed in the churches and assess whether it was geared in any way to the struggle for a new Nicaragua.

One thing all commentators are agreed on is that the numbers of Protestant members and denominations have both been increasing rapidly in the last two decades. The 1980 CEPAD survey referred to in the previous chapter lists seventy-two denominations with a total membership approaching 80,000. It goes on to give further information, province by province, and details the various types of practical Christian work the churches are undertaking, such as literacy, education, health, urban and rural development, and theological education. It also indicates the danger to this work, and to more traditional evangelism, due to the fragmentation process, leading to more and more so-called 'denominations'.

Figures in early 1986 suggested at least another dozen churches had begun since the 1980 survey, though of a total approaching ninety, some twenty are single churches which have split off from other denominations. The number of Protestant adherents in the country is calculated to be half a million, that is around 15% of the population. Pastors are estimated at between 1,800 and 2,200; the term however is a fairly loose one. Any individual can decide that he or she is led to start a new church (or divide one which already exists) and many pastors, even of long-established denominations, have little theological training, little formal education and have never been ordained. Some travel from place to place, in an itinerant fashion. What is clear however is that 99.9% of local pastors are now Nicaraguan, as is the leadership of all the major denominations. Many of the hundred or so North American missionaries who were present during the Somoza era fled to the safety of the USA before or shortly following the Sandinista victory. A few from the mainstream churches remained, despite having the opportunity to leave amidst rumours of a Communist takeover. Growth therefore continues, of Protestant Christians and pastors, but also of new denominations.

The phenomenon of fragmentation is clearly an important one in considering the role of the Protestant churches in Nicaragua. One seasoned Nicaraguan observer pinpoints the causes – at least the internal ones – as *caudillismo*, the incipient 'bossism' of some parts of Latin American society, and the emotional, passionate nature of the people. The former he describes as producing the effect of younger leaders growing up in a fairly large church, or younger pastors building up a following in a denomination, and because of social tradition this then needing to be expressed in a concrete form by breaking out to form a new community with a new leader. The strong sense of the autonomy of the local church in all Protestant denominations also encourages this process. It all leads to a profound spirit of 'Christian free enterprise'. Examples of the above process are an Assemblies of God pastor who after forty years fell into dissent over certain administrative practices of the denomination and led out some congregations to form the 'Christian Mission', also pentecostal, with fifteen churches and twenty preaching places. Another Assemblies of God pastor felt the church had 'lost its sense of spirituality' and that there was a lack of the strong presence of the Spirit, so set up on his own, now having eight churches in his 'denomination'.

A further factor contributing to such divisiveness is the form in which Protestantism has come to Latin America, i.e. at the hands of conservative, North American missionaries who failed to communicate a liberal church tradition, from which in Europe and North America the ecumenical movement evolved. If there is little knowledge or experience of broad-based denominations, which can contain within themselves a variety of beliefs and practices, and which are then able to co-operate fairly easily with other Christians with whose beliefs and practices there is some overlap, then it is not surprising if fragmentation becomes the accepted order of things.

There is now a strong belief among progressive Protestants in Nicaragua that this potentiality among the great variety of denominations for fragmentation, division, conservative theology and anti-Communism has been seized upon and fostered by opponents of the revolution, both inside the country and outside. They feel that the lack of education and of Christian training of many of these congregations and their pastors has been used as a tool by those wishing to undermine the Sandinistas, and the whole process has been exploited by religious groupings set up in the United States for just that purpose, in particular the Institute for Religion and Democracy. We shall return to that analysis later. We now outline briefly the basic characteristics of four of the most important Protestant churches in Nicaragua at the present time, the Moravians, Assemblies of God, Baptists and Episcopalians (Anglicans). We then summarize the work of some ecumenical organizations, including the ubiquitous CEPAD, without a knowledge of which our picture would be very much a partial one.

### *The Moravian Church*

In 1984 the Moravian church reported a membership of 60,000, excluding some 20,000 outside the country who were refugees in Honduras or Costa Rica. This gives a total community estimated at 210,000, with about 150 pastors. The Moravians are a predominantly Miskito church, claiming 95% of Miskitos as part of the Moravian community. There are Creole, Sumu and Rama members, but very few *mestizo* or Spanish-race.

As indicated earlier, the Moravian church is largely to be found in the Atlantic coastal region, stretching from the Rio Coco in the north to the rain forests of the Rio San Juan in the south. There is also a sizeable community in Managua, mostly of east coast exiles. Various languages are used in worship, normally English on the Atlantic coast, Spanish in Managua and Miskito in the internal districts. Because of the preponderance of Miskito members, and because there has been much opposition from the Miskito community to some of the Sandinista Government's policies, the Moravian church has not always been able to interpret effectively the profound social and economic changes being worked towards in Nicaragua.

As was noted in chapter one, the peoples of the east coast knew very little of the progress of the revolutionary struggle until it succeeded. They were then faced with somewhat arrogant approaches from the Spanish-origin west-coasters, who were expecting to be welcomed with open arms by the 'liberated' peoples. The Miskitos however saw all this as potentially another form of the Spanish imperialism which they had been used to in the past, and reacted suspiciously. The Sandinistas – wrongly as they now admit – sought to press the Miskitos into economic, agricultural and political structures they did not understand, and reacted angrily when they made little headway. The Miskitos were then supplied with arms and other military materials by US sources linked with the *contras* and this resulted in a series of armed clashes and in the need for a permanent Sandinista military presence in the north of the east coast region between 1982 and 1984. This situation created deep tensions within the Moravian church, whose leadership had been trying during this period to intercede with the government to take a softer line.

After a good deal of persistence, and also with the urging of CEPAD among others, in 1984 the Sandinistas were persuaded to take a fresh look at the whole problem. During this time the Moravians actually expelled four Miskito pastors for direct participation in the armed revolt, including Wycliffe Diego, who became one of the leaders of the militarized Miskito KISAN group formed in 1985. When however the Moravian leadership tried to press reconciliation too hard they found themselves at serious odds with some of the Miskito membership. Such was the pressure of the situation that the Moravian bishop, John Wilson, felt he had to withdraw from the country for a time. Leaders such as Norman Bent, the Managua pastor who has participated in a number of discussions with government ministers and who is himself half Miskito and half Creole, have maintained that armed opposition to the Sandinistas will lead nowhere, and have attempted to mediate between the Sandinistas and the opposition Miskito organizations.

In this context the SMP (Patriotic Military Service), the Sandinista version of the draft, has posed particular difficulties for the Moravians, partly because the government has been seeking to recruit young men into the Sandinista army who may then have to fight some of their kinsmen from the same racial grouping, especially

Miskitos. Again the Moravians interceded, along with CEPAD, over SMP and the Sandinistas responded fairly sympathetically, at least initially, and in the first part of 1986 were discussing with some of the Moravian leadership how best to proceed.

Although it is a CEPAD member the Moravian church also has its own development programmes, under the auspices of IDSIM, the Moravian Church Institute for Social Development, based in Bluefields and Puerto Cabezas. The Puerto Cabezas office – the origin of the work – was closed down in 1982 by the Sandinistas, but the Moravians persisted and eventually were able to re-open and continue the Institute's work. This includes agricultural development, public health, potable water projects, school buildings, community wharves and emergency assistance for displaced people.

In mid-1986 relations with the state remained delicate, but were improving. The Moravians had asked that any church leaders thought to be involved in *contra* activity be reported to them for action first, but this still was not always happening. In connection with the Triennial Moravian Synod in February 1986 some delegates were reported to have been visited by representatives of state security, making suggestions as to what might be expected from the synod's deliberations. The synod in fact decided to send a delegation to KISAN asking for an end to ambushes and armed clashes in the villages. It also produced a strong statement condemning outside interference and calling on the government and 'those Nicaraguans in armed conflict against the government' to seek a 'responsible and sincere fraternal dialogue', (see Appendix 1 for the full statement). In some parts of the east coast a cease-fire between Miskito groups and government forces had taken hold at this time. Few if any human rights violations by government forces were being reported.

A further matter on the agenda between the Moravian church and the state is that of the 'Autonomy Project' for the Atlantic coast, in which a limited degree of self-government is envisaged for the coastal peoples, in recognition of their special history and culture. The statement adopted at the Triennial Synod recorded 'complete support for the Autonomy process as demanded by the people of the coast'. It also called for all 'to participate actively' in order to achieve a real autonomy in a 'spirit of unity'. Autonomy is a project in which the Moravian church will need to play a full and vital part if it is to have a successful outcome, and to which they are now adopting a much more positive stance.

*The Assemblies of God*

The Assemblies are now estimated to be the second largest Protestant denomination, and the largest on the Pacific coast of Nicaragua. It claims 60,000 members in 500 congregations with about 600 pastors and theological students. Although strongest in the west it also has congregations in the main towns of the Atlantic coast, with both Creole and Miskito members. It is technically independent although the international headquarters of the denomination in Springfield, Missouri, maintain a close relationship with all Assemblies churches wherever they are.

The church is conservative theologically, even fundamentalist, and although initially it welcomed the overthrow of Somoza, when it was realized that the Sandinistas had taken power considerable suspicion began to develop. A few months after the success of the revolution, the head office in Springfield sent down $80,000 worth of books printed in Spanish, stating they were sending a good supply to get them into the country in case 'the doors may be closed'. (In fact this has happened, but by the US Government imposing a boycott, not the Sandinistas.) Duplicating and printing equipment were also promised so that the church would be self-sufficient.

The Assemblies of God remain a full member of CEPAD, although they have made occasional objections to some of the style and content of CEPAD's work. With some others of the evangelical churches they have criticized CEPAD as having become a social agency, even a political institution, rather than a Christian one. CEPAD's response has been that it was set up to do social work, it is the job of the churches to evangelize (although CEPAD believes its work does also result in evangelization). The mild threats to leave CEPAD that have been made illustrate the difficulty a church like the Assemblies has in working ecumenically.

The theology of the Assemblies is biblicist, with strong emphasis on 'what the Bible says' about whichever issue is being confronted by the church. It is also worked out in a context which is heavily North American in ideology, and which therefore includes a strong emphasis on Communism's being part of that evil or demonic threat which is spoken of in certain of the biblical writings. Hence some pastors and members see the Nicaraguan Revolution as part of the fulfilment of apocalyptic prophecy; it heralds 'the last days', just before which there will be earthquakes, wars and rumours of wars, and so on. For a time the earth may be partly in the hands of the anti-Christ, i.e. the atheistic Communists, and this terminology is applied to the Sandinistas in the Nicaraguan situation. In Assemblies' preaching, according to Carlos Escorcia, who is a suspended Assemblies' pastor, there is a subliminal message in which the preacher does not *actually* criticize the government or its intention, but the congregation knows what is really meant. For example a statement such as, 'We are not of the right or the left, we are in the centre,' means that we are opposed to left-wing government and supportive of the parties who refuse to co-operate with the Sandinistas and describe themselves as 'centrist' (while others describe them as being semi-fascist). Again, a statement such as, 'you can only serve one Lord . . . we obey God rather than man . . . the government may have good intentions, but it is only human, and humans make mistakes . . .' is interpreted by the faithful as being critical of the Sandinistas. In an analytical article on the Assemblies, Escorcia comments that after 19 July 1979, the frequent references in Assemblies' pulpits to Romans 13 disappeared, and were replaced by passages like 'it is necessary to obey God rather than man' or 'we serve Christ or the world, we can't serve both', the final part of this text – 'you are not able to serve God and riches' (Luke 16.28) is then omitted![1]

Part of the reason for the denomination's rapid growth, it is suggested, is its willingness to care for the lonely or the new arrival from the country in the big city, and its ability to offer an identity in the amorphous mass of the urban community. In his analysis Escorcia comments that the church does this well, but it somehow then sucks in the new recruit and locks him or her into the church community, rather than liberating people to be themselves. It helps to create moral, upstanding, individual citizens, but does not imbue them with any sense of being a part of their local community, with its Christians and non-Christians, its rich and poor. But he notes that other churches must offer the good things the Assemblies offer, such as a sense of real belonging, if they are going to attract the poor and then work with them towards a new and more positive vision.

After the initial revolutionary enthusiasm had worn off at the beginning of the 1980s, the Assemblies came into conflict with several of their pastors over the church's negative position and by 1985 had suspended six for manifesting support for the revolution. According to the six the church leadership has not dealt with them fairly, preventing a full debate of the charges against them; the leadership has failed even to follow its own rules. Another effect of the denomination's anti-Sandinista stance is that some of those opposing the government for other reasons are joining the Assemblies of God, such as middle-class businessmen and the US Consul, who left a Baptist church in Managua after consistently being opposed by the young people in the church's Bible studies. To Carlos Escorcia this whole process is very sad. He believes that as in the case of the Catholic church the attitudes of some of the leaders are taking the church into the role of political opposition to the Sandinistas; this will drive away the young, who are largely committed to the revolution, and the church will eventually decline and die. Apparently, he says, some Assemblies' pastors believe the Sandinistas are anti-Christian because they seek to feed the hungry, shelter the homeless, give land to the poor, create the 'new man'. Such things must be left to Christ when he comes, say the pastors, it is tantamount to blasphemy to seek to pre-empt what it is for the Lord himself to undertake. There is a deep suspicion therefore, fostered among many Assemblies' members, about the goals of the Sandinista Party, and this does not lead to a very positive relationship. However, the invitation to Luis Carrión, member of the Sandinista National Directorate, to speak at the 50th anniversary celebrations of the Assemblies in November 1986, may herald a different approach in the future.

*The Baptists*

The Baptist church is probably third in size among Protestants in Nicaragua with 7,000 baptized members and a total community of about 28,000. There are some 105 pastors, 64 congregations and 140 'missions' or preaching places. The rate of opening new mission areas has increased rapidly since the revolution. The Baptists also run a hospital, a theological seminary, an old people's home and five schools or colleges. The majority of the membership is Spanish-speaking and found in all parts of the west coast, but there is also Baptist work among the Creole population in Bluefields, Puerto Cabezas, Pearl Lagoon and Corn Island.

There are close relationships with the American Baptist Church (ABC), who also offer financial support, the World Baptist Alliance and the Latin American Council of Churches (CLAI), and in 1983 the Nicaraguan Baptists became members of the World Council of Churches. Pastors and representatives from each church in the Convention are entitled to attend the Annual Assembly, which oversees the training, evangelism, mission, women's and youth work of the church.

When asked about doctrinal emphases of the Baptist church in a magazine interview Tomás Téllez, the Convention's General Secretary, outlined these as belief in the Bible as the unique basis of the faith, baptism by total immersion for all members, the priesthood of all believers, the autonomy of the local church, freedom of individual conscience and the separation of church and state. He saw the role of the local pastor as guide and co-ordinator of the local congregation rather than someone who orders and decides what is to happen, ensuring that the church is non-hierarchical in its practice, both at local and national level.[2]

The Baptists are perhaps the most positive of the Protestant churches in their response to the revolution. Possibly because of the involvement of a number of their young members and pastors in the liberation struggle they have been more aware of the issues at stake and more aware of the aims and intentions of the Sandinistas than other churches.

Jerjez Ruiz of the Baptist Seminary believes that from 1978 the Baptist Convention has had a pastoral body which was intellectually strengthened by graduates from the Seminary. 'They had already received a contextualized theological education,' he says, 'more incarnated in the national situation, and with an ecumenical mentality. These pastors joined with progressive lay-people to enable the Convention to take a direction in accordance with the process of national liberation, which first culminated in the triumph of the revolution in 1979, and still now continues.'[3]

In the interview I mentioned earlier Téllez commented that there are three types of response to the revolution in the Baptist Convention: one which believes Christians cannot be political and are not able to either support or oppose the revolution, another which gives modest support, and a third which, examining the revolution in the context of biblical teaching and the example of Jesus himself, 'supports a process which is bringing benefits to our people and which intends to establish human dignity and a better quality of life'.[4] Téllez rejected the possibility put forward by other Christian leaders (and incidentally the US Embassy) that the Sandinistas are merely biding their time and will seek to destroy religion in Nicaragua in due course. He referred to the numbers of Christians involved in government and the state apparatus. Sixto Ulloa, a Baptist layman and member of the Nicaraguan National Assembly with special responsibility for relationships with the Protestant churches, has a list of over twenty Baptists working at senior levels of government, including at a high level in Foreign Affairs Julio López, one of the original young Baptist pastor supporters of the Sandinistas. Baptist leaders point out that the church has been growing in a variety of ways since the revolution took place.

The environment that the Baptists create in their Assembly, their theological training, even the more modern hymns they sing, shows a considerable awareness of the Christian content in the revolutionary process – both practical and ideological – and a willingness to support it. The church's Education Commission produces a quarterly bulletin of Bible studies for lay leaders and pastors, and the Seminary is just starting an extension course for pastors in more remote areas, both of which take the social and political context in which Nicaragua now finds itself with great seriousness. Asked about Christian-Marxist dialogue Téllez remarked that it is early days yet in the church. 'In Somoza's time you only needed to have a book by Marx or Lenin and you could be informed on, arrested, tortured and even shot. There is still a great fear of "Communism" among our people. There has been some debate initiated by speakers brought in by CEPAD, but it is still primarily among individuals associated with theological training or with institutions like the Antonio Valdivieso Centre.'[5]

The Baptists have made several public statements deeply critical of US policy towards Nicaragua, and have circulated them widely to Baptist churches and ecumenical bodies in the USA and throughout the world. In March 1984, again in November the same year and once more in May 1985 the Baptist Convention opposed the supply of aid to the *contra* rebels and the economic boycott imposed by the Reagan administration. On the occasion of the vote in the US Government in March 1986 to send $100 million in aid to the *contras*, the Baptist Convention sent a telegram: 'In the name of the God of life we urge you not to approve the $100 million . . . (this will) only serve to increase the number of deaths and to intensify the pain of our suffering people. We invite you to support . . . our right to live in peace. May God enlighten you.'

When the aid was confirmed in June 1986 as $110 million, the Convention issued a further pastoral letter to the US Baptist churches, the World Baptist Alliance and all Christians of the United States stating that this decision 'is the advancement of the dominion of the darkness over the light, the imposition of death over life, and force over reason and justice'. The letter goes on to describe the appalling effects of US policy on food supplies, medical care, transportation and unemployment. It refers to the *contra* anti-tank mine which by remote control blew up a vehicle killing thirty-two people of whom twelve were women and twelve children on 3 July. The letter signed by over twenty Baptist leaders continues:

> This aggressive policy of the United States obliges us to live in a permanent state of emergency in order to defend ourselves from

> those who are sending death and destruction. Although this measure is not an obstacle for the work of our pastors and churches, nor for the Nicaraguans who love this country, it does cause difficulties in the development of a normal life. Our prayer to the Lord is that the aggression ceases so that we can live with tranquillity and reconstruct our nation.

It also makes reference to the World Court decision in favour of Nicaragua and against the United States on 27 June 1986, and concludes:

> Conscious of the errors that we as Nicaraguans have committed, and of our role to correct those errors, we ask you as brothers and sisters in Christ and members of His great family, *act so that the United States Government will leave us in peace and will return to us the right to live in peace. Act so that the decision of the World Court of The Hague will be heard and obeyed.* (For the full text, see Appendix 2.)

The Baptists have been willing to risk conflict in their own ranks and criticism from abroad to make their position plain.

### *The Episcopalian (Anglican) Church*

The majority of the 6,000 members of the Anglican church, four-fifths perhaps, are to be found on the Atlantic coast, most of them Creole, with a substantial minority Miskito. The smaller, Spanish-speaking, section of the church is located mainly in Managua and the northern province of Matagalpa. In the past the Anglicans have been the only Protestant church to have regular access to government, partly because the country's three racial groups have more or less equal standing in the church and partly because of the perceived importance of the Anglican Communion internationally. By 1986 the church had twenty-two priests, all Nicaraguan, with about the same number of congregations. After the events of 1979, the then North American bishop fled to El Salvador and the diocese was overseen by the Bishop of Costa Rica. In 1983 however the church formed its own Commission for the election of a new bishop. They eventually chose Rev. Sturdie Downs, of Creole background and originally from Corn Island, and he was consecrated as the first Nicaraguan Episcopalian bishop in February 1985.

The church, which had been in considerable disarray when the revolution took place, began to take some positive if painful steps forward following the 1979 events. It began to see itself as a Nicaraguan church rather than a foreign transplant, and a church which was differentiated from the others by the fact of having in its membership all the country's main racial groupings.

The church indubitably took an important step forward with the founding of the Anglican Institute of the Episcopal Church of Nicaragua in 1982, under the direction initially of a North American missionary, Robert Renouf. This was aimed at training both clergy and laity, and at providing 'critical theological reflection and scientific reflection and analysis on the Nicaraguan church's ministry' along with a framework for debate of social and political issues. It further sought to develop a 'leadership for liberation, autonomy and self-determination' to bring about the 'integration of faith and action'.[6] The present head of the Institute, Rev. Ennis Duffis, who originates from the east coast, says that it is still attempting to pursue this path, although the problems of transportation and the continuing presence of the war create considerable problems.[7]

Two structural issues currently facing the Anglicans are their considerable dependence on foreign funding and their place in the wider Anglican family. They have plans to become financially independent by 1988, but given the severe economic problems of Nicaragua this seems highly unlikely, especially if they wish to retain their present life-style; one observer reports them as being 90% dependent on outside aid. On the second issue a decision in principle was taken in early 1986 to create a separate Anglican Province for Central America, of which Nicaragua will be a founder member.

Ecumenically, Anglicanism has been more progressive in the east than the west, being one of the founder members of CEBIC (the Ecumenical Council of Christian Churches of Bluefields). This led to a good deal of positive co-operation on the Atlantic coast in the 1950s and 1960s which the arrival of the revolution tended to disrupt.

By the end of 1985 things had settled down, and although ecumenism was not as strong the Anglican church resumed most of its former activities. For example it was agreed that St. Mark's would continue as a church school, teaching English and religious education as well as the government's Spanish-based curriculum; the government however took over responsibility for payment of teachers. The main point of tension with the authorities remained the SMP (Patriotic Military Service), the military conscription programme which has been a problem of some magnitude for all the churches on the coast. Some young people had earlier left the country rather than serve in the armed forces, which created pastoral problems as well as political ones. The local priest says however that when the runaways returned they were not punished and have settled down again in the community. He also reported a more open climate for the discussion of the whole issue, including meetings with local Sandinista officials.

There is now slightly more participation by Anglicans in the work of the revolution. One member from the Atlantic coast who joined the struggle of FSLN in 1978 has stayed on and achieved the rank of *Comandante* in the Puerto Cabezas region. Others are involved in the mass organizations, but there is little advice or direction given by the church's leadership as to whether such activity arises from a Christian responsibility. Also, like the Moravians, the leading Anglicans initially refrained from taking an active part in the government's Autonomy Project for the Atlantic coast, despite official requests, preferring to leave the government first to define its project with greater clarity. The church does contain some members opposed to the Sandinistas although this faction does not carry much weight; many of its potential recruits, the more wealthy *mestizo* (Spanish-origin) middle class, have left the country since the revolution.

Politically the Anglican church appears more willing to take up strong positions externally then to engage with the demands being made by the revolutionary process within, despite its potential for bridge-building, both between the different racial groupings, and between the Catholics and the other Protestant churches. It has to be admitted that the latter area has been particularly difficult, given the positions adopted by the Catholic hierarchy; on the Pacific coast the Anglicans say they have for some time only maintained courtesy relations with institutional Catholicism. On external matters the Episcopalian church issued a strong statement from its fifteenth Diocesan Convention held in Bluefields in September 1984, which noted the desire of the Nicaraguan people for peace and the effects of the continual assaults on the country, with large losses in human lives. It condemned 'most energetically' the economic and military aggression of the Reagan administration towards Nicaragua, and called on Episcopal members to try to defend 'with concrete actions' the lives and future of the people. (See Appendix 3 for the full statement.)

In addition Bishop Sturdie Downs has been making some very direct comments to audiences in the United States. In mid-1985, speaking to the Episcopal Church Publishing Company he gave a detailed analysis of the US-Nicaragua relationship, and what this means for Nicaragua:

> For me, the principle cause (of our problems) has to do with the economic interests that the United States has in the hemisphere in which we live. It's not a matter of East-West confrontation. That's what's being said, but that's not what it is . . . It's a struggle of people who have been exploited for too many years by 'the boss' – the one who has never liked to see people develop . . . I'm in agreement with many things our government does, because the government is for the welfare of the people . . . Our problem is one of economic interests. We are the producers, we are the ones who sacrifice. The mighty one in the north takes advantage of our products and the energy of our people. Our people receive no benefits. That's why there is revolution. When there is exploitation, misery, hunger, nakedness, illiteracy and when people become aware – because we are Christian – we find our initiative in the Holy Gospel.[8]

Downs goes on to talk about the effects of the economic boycott, the dangers of the 'capitalist mechanism of consumerism' and the free schooling Nicaragua is now offering. 'If that is Communism then I'm a Communist. And Christ is also a Communist because he was concerned about people, and we must be committed to his gospel.' The bishop ended by saying that unless radical economic measures are taken, especially with regard to the Debt Crisis 'there will be more reasons for revolution in Latin America and in every Third World country. It will also happen here (in the United States). You have exploitation and poverty just as we have in the Third World'. Bishop Downs reiterated these sentiments in speaking to the Washington 'Companions in World Mission' in November 1985. Commenting on land reform he said, 'Before the revolution few farmers owned land and it could be taken away. Today those who work the land have priority . . . and this is right, it should belong to those who work it.' The bishop concluded, '98% of Nicaragua is Christian, and I believe the revolution to be a Christian revolution. We tend to think all the good things are done by Christians, but God uses even those who are not his to carry out his mission.'[9]

With a bishop who makes such radical statements the Nicaraguan Anglicans could be on the move to a much more positive leadership among the Nicaraguan Protestant churches. However it will be necessary to translate such views into dynamic action among the membership, if the church is to contribute effectively to the revolutionary process.

### *Other Christian Organizations*

There are of course many other Protestant churches in Nicaragua but most of the others, except perhaps the Church of the Nazarene, have a tendency towards the kind of fundamentalist theology manifested by the Assemblies of God. Within all these denominations, however, extraordinarily progressive Christians will be found, such as Noel Vargas of the Apostolic Faith church whose story appears in the next chapter, and a pastor from the Church of God in a country area north-west of Managua, whom I interviewed, who started a co-operative in the mid-seventies and was denounced as a Communist by some of the local Somocista land-owners. He had the last laugh; his co-operative took over the estate of one of them when the man fled the country after the revolution succeeded.

However there are also other Christian bodies, all ecumenical to some degree, which are much more important than many of the minor denominations in their influence on and perception of contemporary religious development in Nicaragua. I am offering a list of the more important of these, drawing particular attention to CEPAD and to the Centro Antonio Valdivieso, both of which represent authentic Protestant responses to the Nicaraguan Revolution.

(i) *The Protestant Committee for Aid to Development (CEPAD)* This committee was formed when the churches had made a spontaneous and vigorous response to the 1972 earthquake in Nicaragua, and discovered that they could actually work positively and effectively alongside one another. The human need in the aftermath of the catastrophe, in which thousands died, overcame the mistrust and suspicion which had previously plagued inter-church relationships. Christians recognized their common faith; within five days a committee was formed and three months after the earthquake CEPAD was formally instituted. At that point 30,000 children a day were being fed by 1,200 workers, without one salary being paid. The leadership of CEPAD built on the humanitarian work being done in order to develop a common Christian identity and in 1974 a retreat of 320 pastors from thirty-four denominations was held – the first time such a thing had ever happened in the country. This was known as RIPEN (Interdenominational Retreat for Protestant Pastors of Nicaragua). Local committees of pastors and churches began to organize to try to meet the needs of their communities.

As the Sandinista struggle intensified through the seventies, CEPAD was able to interpret events to some of the more conservative churches, and draw them into a critical stance *vis-à-vis* the Somoza régime. As they worked together on post-earthquake reconstruction and social improvements, the churches became aware of a deeper crisis. As Ruiz and Sullivan put it:

> Little by little the Protestants united in CEPAD realized that development was not going to be a solution for the social problems of the country, without questioning the political system of Nicaragua. Examining the text of the document subscribed to by the

> CEPAD Executive Board of 7 June 1977, a document which arose out of over twenty regional meetings in which more than 800 pastors participated, we see that there is a proposal for a society with open and pluralistic democracy, and a true national integration in geographic and cultural terms, respect for human rights . . . and a genuine Nicaraguan national plan for a definitive way out of underdevelopment and economic dependency.[10]

A few months later, after the assassination of Pedro Joaquin Chamorro in January 1978, CEPAD made an even more vigorous condemnation of the State of Emergency and martial law. There were many close to CEPAD who were not surprised when Somoza finally fell.

At the end of 1986 CEPAD had sixty-seven member organizations, including forty-six denominations, seven religious organizations and fourteen regional pastors' committees, between them representing the great majority of Nicaraguan Protestants. CEPAD now has three main roles according to Director Gilberto Aguirre: emergency relief, a development agency and a kind of 'council of churches'. Emergency relief includes rapid response to floods, hunger and *contra* attacks. As a development agency it operates throughout Nicaragua in four hundred communities, with fourteen programmes including agricultural training, health, housing, education, child welfare, community development, and pastoral studies. It co-ordinates special programmes for the Atlantic coast. It is based at a centre in Managua but has regional offices throughout the country. The full-time regional officers work with the local church committees to decide what types of programmes should be developed and funded in their communities. Hence CEPAD's work brings life and hope to tens of thousands of people around the country. It is probably the largest non-governmental organization in the country in terms of its beneficial effects. 96% of its funding comes from Protestant bodies, some 80% from Europe, including Christian Aid, Oxfam and War on Want in the UK. Its budget is growing rapidly. Donations received in 1984 amounted to $2.4 million, and by the end of 1986 promises of $4.5 million for the 1987 budget had been received.

The CEPAD Assembly, to which all member bodies are invited, meets ten times a year and therefore gives excellent opportunity for democratic participation. The policies, programme budgets, new membership and officers of the organization are all decided on by the Assembly. It is here that the 'council of churches' dimension of CEPAD is most effectively seen, though the varying theological emphases mean that relations are sometimes strained. At one point the Central American Mission actually left CEPAD, only to rejoin later. Even during this period however CEPAD still worked with CAM local pastors, and in fact claims to work with pastors of another twenty-two denominations beyond its forty-six actual members. The Catholic church is not a member, though CEPAD often works with sympathetic priests at local level. It was during 1983 that some of CEPAD's health and education work in the north of the country first came under attack by the *contras*, workers were kidnapped and killed and some projects had to be closed down. The vicious nature of *contra* activities will also be referred to elsewhere.

The relationships with the Sandinistas both at regional and national level have been good since October 1979, when CEPAD called a conference of 500 pastors (RIPEN II) which gave a very positive response to the revolution. Consultation continually takes place with government about where CEPAD can make the most effective contribution to need. The gathering of CEPAD donors in November 1986 was addressed by President Ortega, who also had several members of his cabinet with him. This type of ongoing contact has enabled CEPAD to make representations to government over issues or incidents which have created problems. If for example a number of local church leaders have been picked up in one of the conflict areas by military security, CEPAD has initiated enquiries and representations which have usually succeeded in cooling down situations which might otherwise have increased the tensions in the war zones. Again on larger issues, such as the treatment of the Miskitos in the north-east, or the strict application of the SMP, CEPAD has held conversations with the government continuing over several months, which have eventually led to a more satisfactory approach to the problem. For example, 300 imprisoned Miskitos were released in December 1983 as an indication that the government wanted to start afresh on the east coast problem. The government allows all CEPAD supplies into the country tax-free, and although this happens for all church bodies it is of very considerable assistance for CEPAD's relief and development work.

The work of CEPAD in supporting theological training should not go unmentioned, although the Protestant Institute of Theological Studies (FEET) which it helped to finance until 1986 has now become an independent entity. FEET continues to serve the needs of many of the smaller denominational members of CEPAD, and is located in the Anglican headquarters in central Managua. The new Principal, Dr Benjamin Cortes, a former director of CEPAD, expects the productive relationship between the two to continue.

One criticism of CEPAD has been that the Sandinistas use it as a way to monitor and even control the Protestant churches. Baptist Dr Gustavo Parajón, one of the founders of CEPAD, and its guiding light and current President, rejects this charge, stating that the relationship is one of mutual respect. Parajón says that the government feels free to ask CEPAD's assistance in certain specific ways but CEPAD still feels free to criticize where it believes the government is failing to live up to the high standards it has set itself.[11] Attacks on CEPAD have largely emanated internally in Nicaragua from CNPEN, an organization of pastors we describe below, but also from the Embassy of the United States. Externally the work of CEPAD has come under increasing criticism from reactionary church circles in the United States, particularly the Institute for Religion and Democracy, the IRD. In January 1985 this body published an interview by Kate Rafferty, who claimed to have talked to many Christians in Nicaragua who made allegations about CEPAD's support for the Communist Sandinistas. The article twisted some of the information commonly known about CEPAD's work and made at least one completely untrue allegation, that CEPAD had provided the security police in the Matagalpa region with eleven new jeeps. The mention of the IRD has caused even the mild and saintly Dr Parajón to refer to 'lies and distortions'. In 1986 the IRD was continuing its attacks on progressive Christians in

Nicaragua, apparently as one thread in the Reagan effort to smear anything good or effective going on in Nicaragua, and create conditions for *contra* aid.

The role of CEPAD as both an internal and external interpreter of what is happening in Nicaragua was illustrated at its General Assembly in July 1986. The Assembly had met in response to the US House of Representatives' decision to agree $110 million aid to the *contras*, and endorsed two statements, one to the Protestant churches and the people of Nicaragua, the other to 'The Peoples and Churches of the World'. The first recounted the painful statistics of the 'war of aggression planned and financed by the government of the United States'. The war has resulted in the deaths of 17,000 people; 12,000 children have been orphaned; hundreds of women have been widowed; a quarter of a million people have been displaced and the economic damage which has been done is estimated at over a billion dollars. It proposed a 'Campaign of Prayer and Fasting for Peace', which would be international, and this was also referred to in the second statement. The latter made frequent biblical references in its call to defend 'the orphan, the exploited and the widow' and in its reminder that Christians, citizens of the kingdom of God, 'are called to give good news to the poor, and to proclaim the message of justice, peace and love that comes from the cross of Christ'. This statement also called upon 'our sisters and brothers in Christ around the world to use your spiritual resources so that the war against us – directed by those who make the foreign policy of the United States – will stop'. (See Appendix 4 for the full statement.) Such statements have been extremely useful for Christians outside Nicaragua in counteracting the propaganda promulgated by the United States government.

CEPAD's role in interpretation and communication is greatly assisted by its network of local committees and development projects throughout the country. This enables it, in its public statements and monthly newsletter, to give detailed information about the progress of its educational, health, agricultural and housing programmes and also about the attacks on these life-giving programmes by the US-supplied *contras*. Examples of the latter will be chronicled in chapter four. One recent newsletter gave a detailed report of the changes created in one small community in the northern Jinotega province by the combination of government agrarian reform and co-operative programmes, and CEPAD's health and education work. The same newsletter notes that in communities where Provadenic, the Baptist health programme associated with CEPAD, is active infant mortality is 11 per 1000, compared to 85 in the rest of the country; 69% of children in such communities are free from malnutrition, only 1% suffer severe malnutrition.

CEPAD reports also offer objective information about such matters as the debate on the new Constitution, relations between the government and the Catholic hierarchy, the situation on the troubled east coast and the feelings of Nicaraguan Christians about US government policies. The importance of CEPAD both as an agency for aid and development within the country and as a vital source of information for the outside world cannot be over-emphasized.

(ii) *The Antonio Valdivieso Centre* (CAV) When some of the Catholic and Protestant Christians who had been involved in the struggle for national liberation formed a centre for theological reflection and action in the new Nicaragua they decided to name it after one of the first Nicaraguan martyrs, Friar Antonio Valdivieso, assassinated 400 years ago for his defence of the indigenous people of the country. CAV states that it exists to bring together Christians committed to the revolution to reflect and share experiences, to create a wider movement of opinion, communication and prayer, and to promote Christian unity especially in the service of the poor. It also states its intention not to organize any movement which could be seen as 'competition' by the institutional churches. This reassurance perhaps tells us more about the fears of the Nicaraguan Catholic leadership than it does about the activities of CAV.

The work is carried out by supporting basic Christian communities, training local pastoral leaders, promoting community development projects, organizing seminars and conferences, co-ordinating research and publications and undertaking international solidarity work. The staff at CAV are ecumenical, though as might be expected in Nicaragua, there is a preponderance of Catholics. Most of the Centre's funding comes from progressive Protestant institutions outside the country. There are some thirty staff, most of them part-time, for example local pastors and other church workers.

CAV, like CEPAD, provides programmes for international visitors. Its staff undertake medium-term projects like the organization of the *via crucis* – the 'March for Peace and Life' which Fr Miguel d'Escoto initiated in Lent 1986. It offers a monthly documentation digest in English and a magazine *Amanecer* (Dawn) in Spanish some five or six times a year. The Director is Fr Uriel Molina, parish priest of Riguero, a local *barrio* with a strong tradition of Sandinista support.

The Catholic church in Riguero, Santa Maria y Los Angelos (St Mary and the Angels) is a modern construction with murals depicting events from the revolution integrally linked with biblical personalities and scenes. It is a favourite of foreign visitors with its Sunday evening *Misa Campesina* (a Nicaraguan peasant mass with specially written words and music) though it has close links with the local community also. Molina's identification with the revolution has led to a number of attempts by Cardinal Obando to remove him; in mid-1986 extended 'sick leave' was offered as a compromise.

The theological approach of CAV is a very interesting one. It sees far stronger correlation between biblical events and the happenings and the struggles of the revolution than most other Christian groups. In many ways it comes to almost diametrically-opposed conclusions from those of some evangelical and pentecostal churches, the ones which are suspicious of the Sandinistas for the self-same reasons that CAV supports them. One criticism made of both CAV and Molina is of a too-close identification between the gospel and the revolution: Christianity teaches that human beings, and their institutions, are inevitably imperfect, and the Sandinistas cannot be expected to be a complete exception to that. CAV however seems to believe that they are almost the nearest one can get. This has inevitably caused some conflict with official church bodies.

Nevertheless CAV supplies a particular and important perspective on the Nicaraguan revolutionary process. It offers historical, sociological and theological analysis. It is strongly committed to the revolution and deeply critical of United States' involvement and policy in the Central American region, and it justifies this theologically. One CAV worker commented, 'If the US ever does invade, you can be sure while other church agencies may continue CAV will cease to be. There will be disappearances and assassinations. They won't allow us to survive.'[12]

(iii) *The National Committee of Protestant Pastors of Nicaragua (CNPEN)* This group was initiated by CEPAD in August 1981. It was intended to be a national network which would bring pastors of different denominations closer together, and initiate training and practical support work to assist often uneducated and materially-deprived Protestant pastors. It was funded by CEPAD for its first two years, during which time the parent organization assisted in the preparation of grant applications.

The leaders of CNPEN claim to represent between 500 and 700 of the 1,800 to 2,200 Protestant pastors in Nicaragua, though critics put their membership much smaller, and comment that some people have appeared on the list who did not even know that they were members. The group has a small office housed behind the Bible Society in Managua, and states that it runs training seminars, evangelical campaigns and Bible schools for pastors. It aims to hold an Annual Assembly. Its President says that because it has not yet been granted government recognition as a legal entity its current activities are rather limited.[13] CNPEN has regional committees, although it is not clear to what degree they share the views of the leadership. One CNPEN member, who is an evangelical pastor and a CEPAD regional representative, said privately that although many pastors have been involved with both CNPEN and CEPAD they now find CNPEN's attitude very painful.

Because of what they claim is CEPAD's lack of support, CNPEN leaders have become increasingly critical of CEPAD; for example, there are pastors who accuse it of being uninterested in evangelism. CEPAD's reply is to re-emphasize that evangelism is primarily the responsibility of the churches, but its work supports that of the churches. More potentially damaging however have been accusations emanating from CNPEN circles that CEPAD is controlled by the government, and that politically it has become an arm of the Sandinistas. Such statements created a very difficult relationship which led to a series of meetings during 1985 to try to resolve some of the differences. They have also led to CNPEN being 'adopted' by reactionary forces in the USA. We shall return to CNPEN's role in due course.

(iv) *The Protestant Commission for Social Responsibility (CEPRES)* This body was founded in 1980 by a number of Protestant pastors of various denominations: Baptists, Pentecostals, Nazarenes, and others. It aims to clarify the revolutionary process for Protestants, and organizes conferences, seminars and campaigns around the aims and ideology of the revolution. It is run by a small committee elected from its membership of about seventy who are both lay and ordained. CEPRES publishes pamphlets, produces programmes on radio and TV and has a weekly article in the independent daily *Nuevo Diario*. Its secretary Rev. Roberto Córdoba, a Baptist pastor, says, 'We try to evangelize the churches, they are a great field for evangelization!'

In July 1985 CEPRES organized the first conference for Protestants on the objects and direction of the revolution. It lasted a week, three hundred attended and one of the nine *Comandantes* of the revolution, Luis Carrión, a 'graduate' of the Riguero CEB, gave a keynote address. Testimonies were offered by participants who were active in the mass organizations for women and youth or the Sandinista Defence Committees, and by others who had done their military service in the SMP. CEPRES claims to have collected the names and stories of fifty Protestant martyrs who have died in the service of the revolution since 1978. It has produced a video and a book of the conference. It has working links with CAV, but feels it is good to retain a Protestant identity, enabling it to campaign more effectively among the Protestant churches.

(v) *Association of Evangelical Pastors of Nicaragua (ANPEN)* This is a small group of Protestant pastors which was formed in 1981. At that time it had over eighty members who supported the movement of the masses who were committed to the 'process of the revolution'. According to secretary Oscar Godoy 'we then found ourselves under attack from ecumenical agencies, who did not seem to want an independent pastors' movement with defined support for the revolution'.[14] Godoy, a former Assemblies of God pastor, claims that pressure from these agencies frightened off some of their members, and that the Assemblies even described ANPEN as Sandinista. ANPEN is now closely associated with CAV; it claims to link fifteen progressive congregations in various *barrios* together as a kind of Protestant CEB network and is developing some small development projects to encourage self-help among its members. It aims at an ecumenical and evangelical grouping of churches which will become a new Protestant revolutionary support movement.

(vi) *Ecumenical Council of Bluefields Christian Churches (CEBIC)*
This is the oldest established ecumenical body in Nicaragua, having been set up by its member churches in the 1960s. The founders included the Moravians, Anglicans, Catholics, Baptists and Nazarenes. The latter have now faded from the scene, and although the Assemblies of God have had some discussions with CEBIC basically it consists of the four first-mentioned above. CEBIC began with more traditionally-based ecumenical campaigning work, but after the revolution it suffered severe problems. According to some of the supporters of the time it was used by a small number of articulate Christians actively to plead the cause of the revolution. Atlantic coast Christians are rather conservative in their theology and expect a biblically-based message. Hence some began to drift away, and in 1986 the organization appeared at a rather low ebb.

The Roman Catholic Franciscan Sister who is CEBIC's secretary outlines several possibilities for the future, however. One is a renewal of the joint meetings and services held in better days; another is social or community projects, such as a 'Third World Laundromat' for the women who earn their income by washing. They urgently need proper washing stands constructed, with a clean and hygienic water flow, in order to avoid standing for hours in the non-too-pleasant local streams. A further plan is to develop the twinning arrangement with the London Borough of Lambeth, in which a good deal could be done between the churches of the two communities.[15]

(vii) *The Bible Society* Bible societies, as was mentioned in our first chapter, were quite important in bringing the gospel to Nicaragua in the first place. The Nicaraguan society was founded in its modern form in 1961, but until 1979 it was a stronghold of fundamentalism. After the revolution five board members, whose large land and business holdings had been confiscated because of Somoza family connections, took off for Miami, while the General Secretary – a National Guard general – was jailed.[16] The society is now situated in a pleasant building *Casa de la Biblia* in east Managua. It has ten staff at head office, under General Secretary Ignacio Hernandes, a Nazarene pastor, including two Catholics as well as a variety of Protestants. The Bible Society is a member of CEPAD and participates in their educational and Christian training work.

Although not a supporter of the Sandinistas – he has been quoted as one of their strong critics[17] and was interviewed by the security police in November 1985 – Hernandes admits that the distribution of Bibles since the revolution has gone up astronomically. Between 1970 and 1979 some 9,000 to 12,000 were distributed annually. In 1980 this went to 30,000, by 1983 it was 46,000 and in 1985 it reached a total of 111,000, ten times the pre-revolutionary era. Nearly half of these went to Catholic churches. In addition, up to half a million New Testaments were distributed during the National Literacy Crusade (to a population of only three million). They were requested by Tomás Borge – supposedly the Sandinistas' 'hard man' – and paid for in part by Christian businessmen from the USA. Hernandez says the society has to be careful what literature it distributes in Nicaragua, but agrees there seems to be no problem whatever about Bibles.[18]

(viii) *Eje Ecumenico* The 'Ecumenical Axis' was founded in 1966 by the group of young Baptists referred to earlier, including José Miguel Torres. It was based on the thinking of Dietrich Bonhoeffer and Martin Luther King, and sought a new style of pastoral ministry. It reflected on the armed struggle and the problem of violence, and came out openly in support of the Sandinistas in 1976, the first Protestant body to do so, according to Torres, now its director. He says that after visiting Cuba in 1970 and seeing that the church had become a focus for counter-revolutionary activities he was determined not to let that happen in Nicaragua. He and his colleagues ran Bible studies and seminars seeking to reveal the Bible's commitment to the principles of social justice. Torres was one of the few Protestants linked to the basic Christian communities, in his case Riguero, Fr Uriel Molina's parish.[19]

After the revolution the centre sought to organize meetings and seminars for pastors, and to demonstrate Protestant support at the heart of the revolution. The going was sometimes hard, says Torres, evangelical churches were anxious, dependent as some were on US churches for their survival. The centre tries to continue its work today but for a variety of reasons the resources have diminished and only a fraction of the former work is functioning.

(ix) *Facultad Evangelica Estudios Teologicos (FEET)* This theological institute serves twenty-two Protestant denominations. As stated above, it was until 1986 based at CEPAD, but is now becoming independent. In 1985 there were more than 250 students, across a whole range of denominations, with courses in several areas of theological study. Currently the institute is based in the headquarters of the Episcopalian (Anglican) church, whose students also attend some of the courses of the FEET.

Benjamin Cortes, FEET Principal, reports that he hopes to develop an Institute of Missiological Studies, the first Nicaraguan theological publishing house, and magazines on biblical studies and evangelism. 'The Protestant churches do not need just an understanding of the revolution in the global process,' says Cortes, 'we must also do our own theologizing in our own context. The FEET has a unique opportunity to introduce progressive theological thinking into a wide range of Nicaragua's Protestant churches.'[20]

# 3

# Struggle and Hope – A 'Dawn Theology'

As well as the response of churches and church bodies to the revolution, there are also the perspectives of individual Christians who have sought to participate positively in the struggle, both prior to 1979 and afterwards. There are stories of Catholics which have been told elsewhere, but Protestants have also participated. CEPRES has identified a considerable number of 'Protestant martyrs' who have given their lives to the revolutionary cause, either before 1979 or since. Others, having been long-time members of the liberation movement, are now in government posts, or active in the Sandinista 'mass organizations', which bring together supporters among youth, women and trades unionists, and in local communities in the Sandinista Defence Committees. It is not difficult in Nicaragua to find quite high-ranking government or Sandinista officials who will volunteer personal accounts of a Christian commitment which motivates them to contribute to the ongoing process. This chapter includes contributions, of differing types and lengths, from some Protestant Christians, ending with extracts from a long, reflective essay by Noel Vargas, martyr of the revolution and pastor of the pentecostal Apostolic Faith church, and reproduced at some length because of the insights it offers into evangelical, revolutionary Christian thinking.

### *Laureano Mairena and Solentiname*

Laureano was an officer in the Sandinista army and was killed in action against the counter-revolutionaries on 24 November 1982. He was one of the few Protestants to join the community of

Solentiname, founded on one of the remote islands in Lake Nicaragua by Ernesto Cardenal and William Agudelo in 1966. Laureano himself was born on one of these islands. Before hearing some of his personal reflections on the gospel it may be good to know a little more of Solentiname's history.

Father Ernesto Cardenal, now Nicaragua's Minister of Culture, had wanted when a young priest to join a religious community but was advised by his friend Thomas Merton to begin a new kind of community, committed to living among the poor. For this he eventually chose one of the islands of Solentiname, where the little community spent much time working, worshipping and studying the Bible together in the context of Nicaragua. Their reflections are recorded in the four volumes of *The Gospel in Solentiname*, edited by Ernesto himself.[1] The community found itself drawn towards increasing contact with the FSLN from 1968. Those surviving from the community recount how their study of the Bible brought them to a revolutionary consciousness about Nicaragua's situation, and the need to give more and more support to the Sandinista Front. They had been forced to recognize that it would be impossible to get rid of the Somoza dictatorship without armed struggle.

Eventually a few of the young men from the community, including Laureano, went to Costa Rica for Sandinista military training. When they came back they trained others. In October 1977 the Sandinistas ordered an attack on the National Guard barracks at San Carlos, the nearest town to Solentiname. Laureano and a number of others from the community participated but the attack was a failure and the group had to improvize a difficult and dangerous retreat through bush and swamps across the river to Costa Rica. Two of the young men of the community were killed.

They then lived in exile for some eighteen months until the fighting in the north reached such a pitch that it was clear the end was coming. The FSLN ordered the opening of a southern front, which Laureano and the other Costa Rican exiles joined, and which helped finally to bring Somoza down. Laureano survived. One of his less fortunate comrades was Baptist theological student Sergio Guerrero, killed by a rocket in the fighting.[2] Among Laureano's comments from *The*

*Gospel in Solentiname* are the following:

Commenting on passages on the kingdom of God –

> I am twenty-one;
> I want this new kingdom to happen soon, I don't just want me to see it, I want it to happen in two years . . . The kingdom of God is justice. That is, our only concern must be justice, which is to bring about the Revolution.[3]
> This kingdom that we hope for will come when there's equality, when there's brotherhood. We here (in Solentiname) *do* want the kingdom to come. We're building it . . . If we ask for it we're obliged to do everything we can to make this kingdom come. I mean it comes from God, but it can't be made without us.[4]

Commenting on 'Ye are the salt of the earth, but if the salt loses its taste . . .',

> That's Christianity that has stopped being revolutionary, that has lost its taste.[5]

Commenting on the *Magnificat*, as ascribed to Mary,

> We're divided because the rich divide us. Or because a poor person often wants to be like a rich one. He yearns to be rich, and then he's an exploiter in his heart, that is, the poor person has the mentality of the exploiter . . . That's the revolution, the rich person or the mighty is brought down and the poor person, the one who was down, is raised up. . . . The point isn't that they would just *say* the Virgin was a Communist. She *was* a Communist.[6]

Discussing Jesus with Ernesto, who says,

> I observed that traditionally it has been said that Jesus died at the age of 33, but the gospels don't give his exact age. They say only that when he began his public life he was about thirty, that is a young man, he could have been between twenty and thirty, what we would call a boy . . .
> Laureano (smiling), 'I think he was about my age.'[7]

After his death Laureano Mairena was promoted to be a *Sub-*

*Comandante* of the FSLN. His name has been given to a ship of the Nicaraguan merchant fleet.

### *Olimpia Barajona*

Olimpia is a middle-aged Baptist woman from the north of the country, near the Honduran border. This extract is taken from a personal interview with her in January 1986. She was also one of those who gave her testimony at the CEPRES conference in 1985.

> My grandfather was a general with Sandino in the 1920s. About ten years after Sandino was killed in 1934 my grandfather participated in a new uprising, he was informed on and killed. I was fourteen at the time. Later I married and lived with my husband and children in a village on the Rio Coco. When the struggle began, my husband joined the Sandinistas so I had the opportunity of helping – providing food, acting as messenger, and so on. We supported a particular troop under one *Comandante* for six months, feeding them from our farm. One day the *Comandante* asked if my children could join the FSLN. I told him that as an evangelical Christian I believed we were struggling for a just cause, for which my grandfather had died, so it was in our family blood. So my three sons and one daughter joined. Two months before the revolution succeeded one of my sons was killed in the fighting. Another son continued working for the FSLN and was killed after 1979 in an accident. My other son suffered a broken arm but now works in coffee production for the government. My daughter is with the Ministry of the Interior. I believe our struggle was just and it is precisely because I am a Christian I have participated in the work of the revolution, and I continue to do so. There is no conflict with my faith, rather my work is a testimony to my faith. I am now a member of AMNLAE (the Sandinista women's organization), and a co-ordinator in my town of Ocotal. I am a member of my local Sandinista Defence Committee, and have recently been appointed a member of the district Electoral Council, to represent the Protestant sector. I identify myself in all this work as a Christian, and I believe my words are respected

> because of this. There are Christians who oppose the revolution, that is largely because they are capitalist and their businesses don't earn the same level of profit as they used to. For me the better health, housing, education and land that the revolution brings the people, well, it may be Marxism but it's also Christianity.

A relative of Olimpia's recounted the danger which surrounded her prior to the final insurrection. The National Guard had heard about the work she and her family were doing for the Sandinistas. People were detained and tortured, and 'disappeared' because of such activities. She had to flee in April 1979 to a town further down the Rio Coco until the insurrection. One of her nephews was also killed in the fighting, five days before the revolution succeeded.

### *A Baptist Pastor*

In the period of the final insurrection, which began early in June 1979, there are a number of stories of individual Christians or in some cases whole youth groups who went to the mountains to fight with the FSLN. In some cases this was because the National Guard was threatening to kill all the young males in particular communities. One young pastor, who at the time was still taking his theological studies, tells part of his story:

> I went home to Estelí from the seminary in Managua in June 1979 when the final offensive was beginning. All the youth were being threatened and persecuted so I volunteered for the FSLN. I participated in the insurrection for twenty-five days in the mountains. These days were a really practical way of living out the Christian faith. Sometimes our group had only one *tortilla* (a maize pancake) between us, so we had to break it carefully and equally, like a communion, to share it out. We were very hungry. Many Christian youth were there – Pentecostals, Assemblies of God. You would find Protestants and Catholics praying together in the air-raid shelters.
>
> This whole experience was vital for me. It was as important in a different way as my theoretical and academic training at the seminary. Those who participated in the revolution in this way as

a response to their faith, see things in a different way from most of those who did not. The major difference in the church now is how people understand the gospel. The revolution is posing many challenges to the church – it talks of the creation of a 'new man – or person', of a resurrection in which dead comrades live on in the struggle, of the creation of a really new heaven and earth, here and now. There are many parallels between Christianity and *sandinismo*. It's very important for us to read our Bible in our own context.

### *A Pastor of the Assemblies of God*

This again was a story told in a personal interview in early 1986:

> I became a pastor in the Assemblies of God in 1969. Later I felt it my Christian duty to take up a position identifying with the suffering of the poor. I was told this was a political position, which it was, but everyone here had to take up one political position or the other, for change or against it. Like all Assemblies' pastors I was trained by North American missionaries, for six years in my case. We were indoctrinated with anti-Communism, and I preached vigorously against Marxism, even on buses and in parks, without ever really knowing what it was. In 1973 I went to work in the Matagalpa region, I had thirty congregations of *campesinos*. I saw the repression by the National Guard; they imprisoned, tortured, assassinated – pastors too. This experience taught me it was not sufficient to pray for peace and then do nothing in the face of active persecution. I received death-threats for my outspokenness. Then in 1978 there was a big student demonstration against the Guard, in which my sons were leaders. The church's National Council said this was a bad example and ordered me back to Managua, against the wishes of my church members.
>
> The Guard were increasingly active in Managua, they once took four of my young people from a church youth meeting. We decided to form a Council for Civil Defence in the *barrio*. We organized food, health and housing policy. When the final insurrection started the young people built barricades and organ-

ized our defence. The Guard bombed us and forty-five houses were destroyed. We had to find alternatives for the survivors. I had a personal struggle about whether to take up arms. I don't believe that at that time it would have been a crime.

After the Sandinista victory the ten Assemblies' North American missionaries fled, despite their talk of great faith in God. Our question was, 'Why have they gone?' It seemed to be for political not Christian reasons. I was then an Elder of the Church in Managua, and we brought together fifty Assemblies' pastors to define a clearer position with regard to the revolution and the National Programme of Reconstruction. Then in 1980/1 we began to come under increasing pressure from the Assemblies' headquarters in Springfield, Missouri. At the time of the revolution all church leaders claimed to be revolutionaries. However before long they began to attack the idea of class struggle. 'The Gospel is for all,' they said, 'class struggle is Communism.' Headquarters even came up with $25,000 to fund agricultural projects, so we wouldn't have to participate in the government's programmes. Imagine what the Sandinistas would have thought if we had become dependent on US finance. I opposed such developments.

The denominational leadership then contacted the eight deacons of my congregation and tried to persuade them I was a Sandinista. They succeeded with four of them, and eventually the congregation split. The Board then expelled me, utterly violating our own denominational rules. Our church has a totally 'religious' outlook, spiritualistic, simply about saving souls. They fail completely to understand Luke 4.18. They preach a mutilated gospel.

### *Noel Vargas Castro*

Noel Vargas was a young Nicaraguan theologian, twenty-nine years old, who belonged to the Apostolic Church of the Faith in Jesus Christ, one of the larger Pentecostal churches in Nicaragua. He was killed on 18 October 1982, together with seven teachers and thirty-five *campesinos*, who were massacred by a contingent of counter-revolutionaries who surprised and put to the torch the community of Pantasma in the Jinotega region, destroying granaries, a sawmill, lorries, tractors and office-buildings. Earlier he had written a long reflective article which was published in the magazine *Amanecer* in October 1983. The introduction to the article says,

> Noel sealed with his blood his Christian commitment within the Sandinista revolutionary process, a commitment arising with perfect lucidity from his faith, and expressed as Christian discipleship in solidarity with the cause of the poor. Noel studied in the Latin American Bible Seminary of Costa Rica, and was a poet as well as a theologian. His body was hysterically abused by his assassins, who thrust their bayonets into his unprotected face. But the blood of the martyrs has more power than violence, and will bear fruit. . . .[8]

The following are extracts from the article demonstrating his analysis of the current realities in Nicaragua and his profound belief in the need to integrate the gospel with the revolutionary project in Nicaragua.

> The long oppressive night of our people signifies a long road. A road chosen by a group of young people (i.e. the original Sandinista leaders) when they took a definitive decision in 1961 to embark on a revolutionary process; it was a step from shame to conscience. Also it is a long road travelled by many Christians identified with the bourgeoisie, a road from a dominant and controlling form of religion to an identification with the exploited classes and the oppressed of the country. But above all, this long night is the long road of the centuries which those same exploited classes have had to travel to recover the subversive memory of Jesus of Nazareth from a domesticated gospel. It is for this reason we must clarify for our own existence and Christian conscience that we are ourselves immersed in a process dominated by particular interests . . . For the Nicaraguan situation which today is opening itself up with a new dawn there corresponds a 'dawn theology' . . . Beginning from 19 July 1979, and in real awareness that Christology is interacting with the situation at all its levels the Protestant

church must take on in conjunction with Jesus the situation in which it finds itself, in the same way as Jesus himself took on *his* historical task in communion with the Father and in solidarity with the non-persons, with the oppressed majority of Israel . . . When we come into contact with the historical Jesus we are pointed to the historical power of his programme for liberation (Luke 4.16–21), and its practical implementation (John 10.14–15; 21.15–17). This historical Jesus is the disturbing sign of all liberating practice, and is the horizon opened to all prophetic carriers of a liberating project.

The fundamental characteristic of the announcement of the kingdom in the historical person of Jesus is its eschatological character. But it is an announcement also made in words and deeds. The eschatological announcement unleashes a crisis, in the moment and in humanity, in which Jesus offers the true identity of humanity through conversion, without which the kingdom does not happen . . . The kingdom of God posits essentially a future dimension, but it is not solely futuristic and utopian, it is also present, and as such finds itself expressed in *sandinismo* and in the whole process of liberation in Nicaragua. It is a process which begins in the world and culminates in the final 'eschaton'. In Jesus is maintained this dialectical tension: the project of total liberation (the kingdom of God) and the historical mediation which is fulfilling it (revolution).

By means of the activity (the visible signs) of the disciple of Christ, God installs this kingdom. It is concretized in human beings, who perform in a specific way with their fellow creatures, disinterestedly helping and serving them . . . This is because in the historical practice of Jesus one does not reach God essentially through worship, nor through religious observance alone. He is reached above all through the service to the poor in whom, anonymously, He reveals himself.

The political death of Jesus establishes a discontinuity with his own life. What was declared as hope, at the end of his life only shows signs of failure. But he is not a political or religious martyr among others, who die as part of their message. No, the God he was preaching and whose nearness he was announcing abandoned him. In the crux of the abandonment Jesus exclaims with a great cry of protest from the Cross, 'My God, my God, why have you forsaken me?' Moltmann (and others) have interpreted this cry as revolution in the concept of God. In the Cross the images of God are broken and that God dies to give way to a God with no 'image', to a greater God . . . The Cross and the death of Jesus are described as a total questioning of the way towards God . . . To know God from the Cross is a radically new way of knowing the Father of Jesus Christ. Bonhoeffer has captured it perfectly in saying that to know God is 'to stay constant with God in his passion'.

The historicity of the resurrection is not only an isolated act in which a certain Jesus of Nazareth rose from the tomb, nor is it just that he appeared among certain of his followers. To understand the historicity of the resurrection of Jesus is to relate it to the historicity of the primitive Christian communities which were shaped in the light of this historical certainty of the rising from among the dead. . . . From the resurrection God is revealed as liberator from the tyranny of death just as in the Exodus he liberated his people from a historical tyranny. It is not enough that individuals as such are resurrected, what the fullness of the kingdom essentially implies is the creation of new human beings living in community under 'a new heaven' and on 'a new earth' where justice dwells.

Finally, if the Cross is not the last word on Jesus because God raised him from the dead, and if the resurrection is not the last word on history because God is still fulfilling it, then 'in the piece of history which we are living today in Nicaragua Christianity has before it the perfectly Christian possibility of interpreting this history, inasmuch as it leads towards justice, towards solidarity, towards the interests of the poor, for whom God in Christ showed his preference. Christianity has every right to interpret it as history under the sign of the Spirit' (Juan Hernandez).

The dawn is not synonymous with the end but rather with a fresh beginning; today we have begun afresh to hold a historical confidence and faith in the God of the poor whom Jesus revealed to us. For that, with Christ, as the people of God we want to reaffirm that from the paschal joy of the victory over the dictatorship we are going to take on our new historical task of being followers of Jesus Christ in this new Nicaragua.

Today, after the second Sandinista popular insurrection – the National Literacy Crusade – and by way of embarking upon new and greater insurrections, we have to incarnate our Christological faith within the face of the Popular Sandinista Revolution, in theological opportunity and temporal anticipation of the kingdom for which Christ lived to the ultimate. To affirm our faith in the revolution and in Jesus signifies a living of both scandal and anathema, according to the view of the 'professionals' of the Temple and the Law. In fact the Nicaraguan Democratic Movement (the *contras*) and the reactionary sectors of private enterprise cannot conceive that the project of economic independence over against the imperialists is totally Christian. Neither do they believe it is possible for non-believing revolutionary practice to come together with Christian revolutionary practice, not just at the level of a strategic alliance, but at the level of revolutionary unity.

Finally we believe that in Nicaragua today, not to read the gospel and not to follow Jesus in a form both liberating and liberated is to understand the gospel in reverse, and to interpret it in an ideological form which serves new forms of oppression. To announce the kingdom as antagonistic to the Popular Sandinista Revolution, or to preach it as concretized in the church, its worship and dogma, its institutions and sacraments, is to withdraw from the task of expanding the kingdom. That is to say it is to deny the historical presence of the God of Jesus Christ in the blood of thousands of brothers and sisters who have fallen believing in the historical power of the oppressed classes of Nicaragua. It is evading irresponsibly the task of reconstructing our society, of renewing the economy, of increasing the educational level of our people, of activating the gospel and consolidating the human achievements of this revolution which is, except for the oppressors, for all.[9]

These extracts are representative of the thoughts and reflections, the actions and sufferings of some Protestant Christians and their families as the revolution evolved. Other stories are available in the report of the 1985 CEPRES Conference. As we have already said, there was little comprehension of revolutionary expectations in the churches as institutions. But among some individual Christians there was a profound sense that the revolution was a 'kairos-time' for the faith, a time for struggle, for hope, and in some cases for a willingness to carry their cross, to pay the ultimate sacrifice. It was also however a time of dawn, and the 'dawn theology' of which Noel Vargas wrote, clearly epitomizes something of great importance for many Protestant Christians engaged in the Nicaraguan revolutionary process.

# 4

# Engagement and Opposition – Response to Revolution

It seems at this point appropriate to offer an account of what the Sandinistas are trying to do, what the revolution is actually attempting to achieve. Clearly it is seeking to bring fundamental changes to Nicaragua, a project which draws diverse responses from Christians in the various churches, or even in the same church. It is a polarizing process. It divides members within families as well as within churches. Is what is being attempted worth the trouble, the separation, the suffering caused? Having outlined the project of the revolution, I will then examine the churches' response in practical terms, going on in the later sections of the chapter to look at the growth of the religious opposition and the activities of the counter-revolutionaries, the *contras*.

## *The Project of the Revolution*

Latin America has remained, despite all the efforts of the last 400 years an 'underdeveloped' sub-continent. That term itself is a loaded one; to some it is a statement of fact, to others it describes a process which is the direct result of economic relationships. Fundamentally however it means that vast numbers of the peoples of Latin America have remained poor, dispossessed, ignorant, unhealthy, landless or unemployed. For 150 years the region has been subject to the North American system of finance and trade, but despite numerous promises and commitments, the poor have either stayed the same or got poorer. The social class structure has remained, with a small number of wealthy business, landowning and political leaders in positions of power, and although peasants' and workers' movements have arisen they have had little general influence, and certainly none in changing basic structures or redistributing the continent's considerable wealth.

In Central America the problem is even more stark, with the countries having little in the way of natural resources and having geographically been under even closer US control. In Nicaragua this meant until 1979 a small 'ruling class' of land owners and businessmen closely linked with the political and military leadership (nominally differentiated as 'liberal' and 'conservative'), a small working class mostly confined to the towns and cities, and employed in processing, manufacturing or service industries, and a large number of *campesinos* living in the rural areas, some with their own land but most having to work all or part of their time on land owned by others. The economy was heavily linked to the US, in the sense that all machinery, inputs (from cloth to fertilizer), technical knowledge, fuel and even a proportion of capital came from there. There was no linkage between the different sectors of the economy; for example there was hardly any metal industry so repairs to machinery or spare parts depended on US sources. The crops produced were dictated by world market prices, and had nothing to do with the nutritional needs of the people; for example coffee was regarded as much more important than beans, the staple nutrient for the *campesinos*. The minimum in terms of an education or health service was being offered to the people. On one occasion when the dictator Somoza was being shown health centres in Costa Rica he was heard to observe, 'We don't need such things in Nicaragua, we don't need people, we need oxen.'

It was therefore clear to the Sandinistas and their supporters that basic and fundamental changes were needed in their country, both in its priorities and the economic structure. As is well known by now, one of the first mass activities they undertook was the National Literacy Crusade when for six months in 1980 100,000 school students and other volunteers spread out into the shanty-towns, the country villages and the rural communities to teach people to read. Many local churches participated in the campaign. That programme continues in a different fashion, but close behind it came the health campaign tackling hygiene, diet and drinking water problems, and diseases such as polio and tuberculosis. After six years of such programmes the infant mortality rate had been driven down from 130 per 1,000 to 78, life expectancy rose and polio was almost wiped out. Vaccination campaigns continue regularly throughout the country. If parents fail to bring their children to the clinics the nurses and health volunteers go out to find them. There might seem to be parallels with the parable of the Lost Sheep in the methods of the Nicaraguan education and health campaigns.

Housing has been another priority where attempts have been made to re-house many of those living in the one-room, wooden 'orange-box' constructions which are such a feature of 'Third World' towns and cities. A senior housing spokesperson has said that by early 1986 the housing ministry was working with 300 of the 420 communities nationally in which it needed to be active. By the end of 1985 new housing had been constructed for 20,000 family units, and the annual rate was 160,000 square metres, each unit being 40 square metres. Many poor people were given, at low rents, houses which after twenty years would become theirs. Some of the housing had been constructed by the poor themselves from materials supplied by the government. But perhaps most important of all, people were being given a title to their land so that for the first time the land and the house on it was legally theirs. This is also being undertaken for housing already existing. Sadly by early 1986 the programme was having to be reduced because of the costs of the *contra* war.[1]

Housing and land policy is a symbol of the more fundamental intention of the revolution, to shift ownership, control and responsibility to the people, and away from those who held it all before. One crucial problem of all poor countries is land ownership, and in many other South American countries possession of the land is passing inexorably into fewer and fewer hands, either individuals, local companies or trans-national corporations. In Nicaragua the two Agrarian Reform Acts are designed to put land into the hands of the *campesinos*, in some cases for the first time. This has partly been possible because when Somoza and some of his supporters fled in 1979 their land was seized by the government, and was available to be redistributed to *campesinos*. The Sandinistas inherited 23% of the land in this way. Other land was purchased in an agreed manner from its owners, and the second Agrarian Reform Act further provided for the expropiation of idle lands remaining uncultivated for two years or being insufficiently used. A full and useful account of the Agrarian Reform process is to be found in chapter two of *Nicaragua: A Revolution under Siege.*[2] By July 1985, 70,000 families had received land, either individually or in co-operatives. At the beginning of 1986 the Sandinistas began to turn the screw on landowners who for political reasons refused to sell some of their land, though they had already received very adequate offers, and in communities where there were many *campesinos* without land some land was being expropriated. A further crucial aspect of agrarian reform has been the instruction to banks – now nationally-owned – to give credit to 120,000 *campesinos* where before many had no such access.

In the areas of agricultural production and marketing of key exports such as coffee, cotton, tobacco, sugar and fruit the government is encouraging owners to produce to the maximum, while itself controlling the price they are paid within the country. Hence the government now absorbs excess profits for the benefit of the people as a whole, and big landowners are restricted to 20% to 30% profit. They have to justify their purchases of inputs or machines, as these must all be paid for in the precious dollars of which Nicaragua has all too few. In the agro-industries and in manufacturing, workers are being encouraged to take a much greater interest in the way things work, to report abuses of their company if such occur and to seek to ensure production remains at the maximum for the good of the community and the country. As workers themselves still have no real control or ownership it is not always easy to persuade them to do this. However the Sandinistas have clearly stated their wish to retain a mixed economy, and indeed the bulk of the land and 60% of production remains in private hands (roughly the same proportions as in 1979).

When it came to power in 1979, the new government offered guarantees to the private sector that their enterprises would be offered the opportunity to play a major part in economic development. It stated its view that to nationalize all the means of production in an underdeveloped economy would lead to 'destruction and disarticulation'. Hence between 1980 and 1982 54% of government credits were granted to the private sector against 46% to the state sector. Despite the fact that many of the biggest land and factory owners fled the country after Somoza's downfall, in 1982 large private producers still accounted for over 50% of production in the key agricultural and manufacturing sectors. The private sector could have an even greater influence in the economy, but many producers are sitting firmly on the fence and keeping their money in foreign banks. A World Bank report in 1982 noted that the weak recovery of the Nicaraguan economy was largely due to private sector failure to expand production and invest in the country's development. In particular poor export performance has caused a grave shortage of foreign exchange. If the private sector continues to avoid its responsibilities in this area, expert observers say the government may have to intervene in the economy to a degree it had hoped would not be necessary.[3]

Because of the effects of the war, the continually low prices of agricultural products in the world market and the economic boycott by the USA (which also prevents loans from international funding agencies to Nicaragua), the economy is entering a stage which is now being described as a 'survival economy'. This requires planning to ensure the *campesinos* have enough land to feed themselves and, with the larger landowners, enough spare capacity to feed the rest of the population. It means a halt to the credit provided to business, which until 1986 had largely been dependent on government money.

The business sector has of course been the most critical of the Sandinistas, and the least willing to put its own considerable wealth forward for the nation's benefit rather than its own. One young western economist working with the government commented in disgust on the unwillingness of businessmen to invest. 'Now there's no longer a government credit cushion,' he said, 'they'll have to either put in their own capital or else close down. Some will probably contribute but others will just follow their friends to Miami.'[4]

Another young economist working for a church agency spoke of the way his studies in Nicaragua had changed his perspectives.

> I have had to begin to look at my economics much more from a biblical perspective. Economics ought to be based on how the poor are doing; without a high degree of equality in a nation neither economic nor spiritual health is possible. Economics should be about producing sufficiency for all, not consumerism for the wealthy. Per capita income in Nicaragua is the same as it was twenty years ago, which isn't bad, despite the 1972 earthquake and the 1982 floods and drought – the worst ever. I believe that still the poor have more hope in Nicaragua than in any other Central American country.[5]

Finally something needs to be said about the political structure in the aftermath of the revolution. The Sandinistas claim to be seeking to maintain a pluralistic democracy, and certainly the election held in 1984 was felt by most observers to have been one of the fairest ever in Central America. The Sandinistas obtained 67% of the vote, the six other parties – three from the right and three from the left – obtained 33% and certain other parties withdrew claiming unfair practices. United States agencies were active in encouraging parties not to participate, they offered money in some cases and appear to have instructed their presidential candidate Arturo Cruz not to run when it became clear he would be heavily defeated.

As in any Western-style democracy the party with a very large majority gets its own way most of the time. However according to local church observers the government remains open to constructive cricitism from its friends. The most important current political project is the new Constitution, and the churches have taken an active part in the discussions on this, through debates arranged by CEPAD (see below).

One question which the Sandinistas have on the whole refused to answer is whether they would leave office gracefully if 'voted out'. They claim such a thing could never happen anyway. It has to be noted however that such other 'democratic' structures as exist in Central America, for example in Costa Rica and El Salvador, do not offer any real alternatives in their political parties, and that it is impossible in most such countries to undertake a genuine political debate anyway, because as soon as a socialist alternative appears to be succeeding, the power of the reactionary forces, in particular the military, is brought to bear. The true nature of such forces can be clearly observed in the events of 1973 in Chile, when a democratically-elected government was overthrown by big business interests and the military sector, backed and co-ordinated by United States government agencies.

### *The Churches' Response*

The most representative view of the response of the Protestant churches to the aims and objectives of the revolution is probably obtained from CEPAD, although CAV and CEPRES speak for a number of groups also. It is CEPAD which acts on behalf of the Protestant churches in such practical areas as housing, health and education. It should be said first that CEPAD is categorical in its support for the practical aims of the Sandinistas in the social dimension. 'We are quite clear that where the government is working for the improvement of conditions of the poor we will work alongside them,' says Gilberto Aguirre, CEPAD's Director, 'and we believe this government is committed to the poor.'[6] Hence the CEPAD departments, which cover the whole range of social welfare, usually plan and co-ordinate their operations in conjunction with the relevant government departments at national and local level. CEPAD says its resources are best used in this way, and it is supported in this view by the international aid agencies who fund it. One local aid representative has declared that, dollar for dollar, aid has been much more effective in Nicaragua than most other Latin American countries because of the positive attitude of the government, and the co-operation between the government and CEPAD.

Because of CEPAD's unique position, both inside the country and internationally, the role of interpreter and communicator of government social policy has fallen upon the organization. Internally it has held conferences and seminars, partly to develop the perceptions of its own staff and its church representatives, but it normally invites government spokespersons also, to explain the government's current thinking, and respond to questions or criticisms. Two concrete results of this process are the CEPAD reports *Reflexiones sobre Fe y Revolución* (Reflections on Faith and Revolution) 1982, and *Reflexiones sobre Paz y Realidad Nacional* (Reflections on Peace and the National Situation) 1983. An example of the kind of thinking behind these reports comes in a paper from the latter on 'The Mission of the Church in Nicaragua Today' by staff member Albino Meléndez, in which he seeks to show biblically that salvation includes the physical as well as the spiritual. He also sees mission as the 'full humanization of humanity' and as participating in the activity of liberation. He points to the way in which the old economic and class structures can prevent this, and thus assists untrained pastors and lay leaders to undertake more cogent theological and social analysis.

CEPAD has also called together large conferences of pastors from all its member churches from time to time – the events known as RIPEN. The first RIPEN event was held in 1974 before the revolution took place, and the second three months after it, in October 1979. The fourth took place in April 1986, when seven hundred pastors from seventy-six denominations gathered for five days of meetings, workshops and worship. Coming from almost every part of the country the pastors studied the themes of church growth, biblical interpretation, pastoral psychology and the work of the Holy Spirit. They reflected also on the life of their churches in a country 'suffering foreign aggression and a crippled economy'.[7] CEPAD sees part of its work as introducing the often untrained pastors to other streams of theological and sociological thinking, so visiting speakers and resource people are a part of the RIPEN conferences. At RIPEN IV President Daniel Ortega also attended to give an address and answer pastors' questions. He began his address by saying,

> Our first desires to do something for the Nicaraguan people were born within our Christian formation and teaching . . . (the Sandinistas saw) Christianity at the side of the people . . . We saw Christ united with the poor and not defending the rich. We saw

> Christ struggling even willing to give his own life, for the authentic liberation of humanity.[8]

The pastors then put questions to Ortega including why the Catholic church continues to get special treatment, why some local government officers do not co-operate with local pastors' development committees, the problems of the SMP, the detentions of some Protestant Christians and the government's efforts to solve the country's economic problems.

Another example of CEPAD's activity in the communication field is its annual report, which helps to explain some trends to outside observers. The director's introduction to the 1984 report, for example, offered a detailed analysis of the national economy, demonstrating why the country is currently suffering severe economic problems. It described the Nicaraguan government's efforts to concentrate on unemployment, interference by the US in the attempt to obtain international loans, the drop in investment, shortage of foreign exchange, worrying ratio of imports to exports (2:1) and rapidly increasing foreign debt. It then explained why the devaluation of the local currency took place to deal with all this, commented that this also affected CEPAD in its relief and development work and pointed to the culpability of the North American administration. The director concluded with an assurance that 'the Lord will be with us', and quoted Psalm 145.[9] It was yet another example of how Nicaraguan Christians view their suffering in the context of international economics and biblical teaching, and how their faith seems strengthened rather than weakened by adversity.

The position of CEPAD with respect to the Sandinistas could be described as one of 'critical solidarity', a phrase used by some eastern European Christians. This enables it both to offer constructive criticism and to act as community peacemaker when the occasion demands. Both of these can be very positive roles as the revolutionary project unfolds. One example of the former is the involvement of CEPAD, with and alongside individual Protestant churches, in the debate on the new Nicaraguan Constitution. It contributed to the first draft while it was still being drawn up and then when it was published participated actively in the ongoing discussions. The agency produced a half-page advertisement of its comments, which was published in the Sandinista newspaper and the independent daily, but refused by *La Prensa*, the US-sponsored newspaper which was closed down by the government in July 1986 for exactly that kind of confrontational attitude. In June 1986, *cabildos*, or open forums, were held throughout the country for Christians to comment on the Constitutional draft. One of the main arguments was whether God should be mentioned in the Preamble; this was opposed on the grounds that many governments in history had simply used God to legitimize oppressive rule, and 'with a healthy separation of church and state in Nicaragua, God would be better left out of the Constitution'. In the end, God was left in, but purely in the context of a recognition of those Christians who participate in revolutionary struggle because of their faith.

When the National Assembly debate on the Constitution was completed in November 1986, the CEPAD Newsletter carried an interview on its implications with the agency's legal adviser, Baptist Dr Adolfo Miranda. He noted first that the new Constitution reflects the particular nature of the Nicaraguan Revolution and does not follow a Soviet or Cuban model. It guarantees the rights of all political parties to participate in free elections every six years. Miranda also says that, given the provision for proportional representation, the new Constitution is more democratic, participatory and pluralistic than the US Constitution. When asked his view as a Christian Miranda comments that complete religious freedom is guaranteed but that more importantly the rights of the oppressed, the poor and the exploited are guaranteed. On the vexed question of the SMP and conscientious objection Miranda states firmly that the constitution does not oblige Nicaraguans to take up arms to invade another country, it calls for military service only when the country itself is being invaded; further, one can participate in military service in a medical capacity or as a cook, a janitor, an office worker, and so on. He believes the door has now been left open by the Sandinista government to conscientious objection.[10]

Another example of the role of constructive critic has been the very troubled debate over the Atlantic coast situation, and the breakdown of relationships between the Sandinistas and much of the east coast community during the period 1981 to 1984. CEPAD's persistence, together with some Moravian church leaders, in pointing out the problems in the revolution's approach to the east coast, and in helping to create alternative methods of dealing with it, has been a positive initiative. Some on the Atlantic side still see *mestizo* Sandinista attitudes as racist and imperialist; one senior churchman who has had much to do with trying to resolve this particular issue was clear that these are both present. But with goodwill on both sides, continued involvement by CEPAD and a more active commitment from the east coast churches, a solution which will genuinely benefit the east coast peoples is achievable, provided the United States is not destabilizing the process.

Beyond the immediate work of confidence-building and peace-making on the Atlantic side lies the Autonomy Project, in which CEPAD, the Moravians and the other east coast churches have been invited to play an active part. Some local church leaders are already involved. For example the Baptist minister in Puerto Cabezas is co-ordinator of the local Ecumenical Commission for Peace and secretary of the zonal committee of the Autonomy Commission, and the head of the Moravian College in Bluefields is a member of the full Autonomy Commission. The active and positive participation of the churches can make a vital contribution to resolving the problem of the coast. The basis evolved in 1986 for autonomy was an elected assembly for the region, representatives to the National Assembly, a proportion of the east coast's resources to be at the disposal of the local assembly, and shared local responsibility for the economy, education, land-ownership, health and other vital aspects of the community's life. Some Miskito leaders are still proposing total local control but most church leaders in the east recognize that this is not a viable possibility for the government in sovereignty terms, and continue to emphasize that 'we are all Nicaraguans'.

In terms of 'peace-making' generally in the country, CEPAD has been able to assist on a number of occasions. One example was the occupation of three evangelical churches in a Managua *barrio* in

1982 when young Sandinista militants took direct action against churches which were said to be actively preventing their members from participating in community activities. These churches were said to be not just neutral but supportive of the counter-revolution and it was reported also that 'North American military books' had been found in one of them. A similar incident occurred in the north Matagalpa region, mostly directed against Catholic churches, but on each occasion CEPAD was able to intervene and conciliate.

A further case arose in early 1986 when, as part of the security action against the *contras* in the Chontales area, a large group of civilians was detained for questioning, including a number of evangelical pastors and students. The president of CEPAD travelled personally to the scene, to meet with both the security authorities and the detainees, to encourage the latter and to press the former for a quick resolution of their enquiries. It was the type of situation which could have become damaging both at local and at international level. There is nothing that some western commentators enjoy more than Communists arresting Christians in Nicaragua. However, it does need to be said that sometimes church members have been active in support of the *contras*, and CEPAD is aware of that too.

Another type of intervention has been that on behalf of individual pastors who have been detained for questioning, such as the six evangelicals picked up in November 1985. These were some of the CNPEN leaders I referred to in chapter two, and included some of CEPAD's worst critics. Nevertheless representations were made, and the release of all the pastors was obtained relatively quickly.

Another area in which CEPAD and some of its member churches have been active in negotiation with the government has been that of the SMP. As I mentioned earlier, a number of churches were troubled by its introduction, and manifested objections on grounds of conscience. It says a good deal for the Sandinistas that they were prepared to discuss the whole issue with the churches. Other governments in the region would be highly unlikely to negotiate over such crucial aspects of military strategy. However CEPAD and its members have obtained certain concessions for Christians conscientiously unable to take up arms, and have facilitated a move towards the adoption of the concept of conscientious objection for perhaps the first time by a Latin American government. This debate has also borne fruit in the final form of the new Constitution, though the subject remains an important area of debate between the churches and the government. Father Miguel d'Escoto, commenting on the war and the need for the draft, calls it 'a gospel concession to a world in transition'. The Christians in government see it as an unfortunate necessity. One result of the dialogue may have been to limit the numbers of people leaving the country, since with no possible alternative to military service better-off Christians had been sending their children out. In some cases whole families were departing, either to neighbouring countries or to the USA. Thus CEPAD and its member churches have contributed in a number of ways to sensitizing the revolutionary process.

Apart from the work of CEPAD there are churches and other ecumenical organizations which are making an actively positive response to the revolutionary project. In the Baptist church there is a serious attempt to ensure that theological training at all levels takes place in context, so that biblical, historical and doctrinal studies for student pastors and lay leaders are grounded in the contemporary Nicaraguan situation. The church holds special seminars from time to time: there was a widely-advertized series of six in late 1985, and in March 1986 the Baptist Seminary hosted a series of meetings by the radical German-American theologian Dorothée Soelle. At local level some Baptist congregations run community projects in conjunction with the local political authorities. Gennesaret Baptist Church in the Managua *barrio* of San Judas has a nursery school for 120 children, holds adult education classes in the evening and co-ordinates the Martin Luther King Co-operative Project to make roofs for poor families in local *barrios*. The First Baptist Church in Corinto works with CEPAD on housing, agricultural and health projects, and has formed the first Protestant-Catholic ecumenical group, with both a religious and a practical content. As well as meeting for prayer the group has obtained a piece of land for three poor families to grow their own food, and started a sewing co-operative for five women, both Baptist and Catholic. The Corinto church has linked up with the local hospital, providing Bibles and also water for the patients during the day, a necessary item in a country where clean water supplies are a continuing problem. The local pastor comments that after forty years of a right-wing government where the church could do nothing it was refreshing to be able to undertake some positive action.[11] Many Christians participate in the co-operative movement, especially in the north where *contra* activity makes it necessary both to join a co-operative and to take up defensive arms. So while many local churches continue to view politics with some suspicion, others are rolling up their sleeves and 'doing the gospel'.

Organizations like the CAV and CEPRES also seek to respond positively to the Sandinista project, largely in the field of education. They seek to interpret the government's aims and intentions to the Protestant people, and to offer training in communications and community development through seminars and conferences. They offer a rather sharper historical and theological analysis than CEPAD is sometimes able to do; the latter always needs to pay attention both to its internal constituency and to its overseas donors. They also provide a forum for those Christians who wish to be radically involved with the revolution, and committed to it in a way which is still quite difficult within the mainstream churches. In addition CAV has frequent foreign visitors who are able both to give and receive from the new Nicaragua in a theological context. For example, one visitor spending a week there in March 1986 was Father Betto, Brazilian Dominican author of *Fidel and Religion*, a book based on his interviews with the Cuban president on the role of religion in Latin America, which has proved enormously popular throughout the sub-continent.

At an individual level there are many Christians now in positions of responsibility in government. Most are Catholics but among the Protestants are Julio López in the Foreign Affairs Ministry, Sixto Ulloa and Dr José Marie Ruiz in the National Assembly, the Ambassador to Austria and the First Secretary to Belgium in the diplomatic field, other Assembly members originating from various churches, and *Comandantes* Cuthbert and Campbell in the east coast region. Many Protestants are members of the Sandinista mass organizations. But other factors have to be taken into account; for example Protestants are hardly 15% of the population, many of them are on the troubled east coast and the Protestant churches, as we have heard, did little to prepare their members for the revolution. An individual example is Baptist Sixto Ulloa. He began as an opponent of Somoza in the seventies who offered humanitarian assistance to the Sandinistas. This came to the knowledge of the death squads who at one point forced him to leave the country, although he says he could not retreat from the struggle for long and soon returned. As a member of CEPAD, after the successful final insurrection he acted as a link-person with the new government. In October 1983 he received an invitation from the FSLN to stand as a representative for a Managua constituency in the 1984 election, though he is not a member of the Sandinista Party. He says his work as a member of the National Assembly is certainly an out-working of his Christian faith. He acts as a link with the Protestant churches and declares categorically that there is no threat to the churches, either now or in the future, unless they allow themselves to be used by counter-revolutionary elements against the interests of the Nicaraguan people.[12]

Hence there is a wide range of positive response to the revolution among Protestants, speaking institutionally, at local church level and among individuals. There are also however those who take the opposite attitude.

### *The Religious Opposition*

As I indicated earlier in the discussion of the CNPEN group there are some evangelical pastors, and even some Christians in the mainstream denominations, who have exhibited suspicion and even opposition to the revolutionary project. In general the activities of the group in the mainstream churches are contained within their denominations. The problem is a little different for the Moravian church, which has a fair proportion of its Miskito members either in exile as refugees or organized in active opposition to the Sandinistas. It should be said that their action was taken not with a specifically

Christian motivation, but to defend the cultural and economic interests of the Miskitos, including the possession of their land. During 1985 there was a softening in the Sandinista attitude to the rebel Miskitos. The former are now no longer described as *contras* but as 'indigenous people who have taken up arms' to defend their interests. In fact, the Moravian church is a 'peace church', and one factor bewailed by some of the Moravian leadership is that – because the Atlantic coast had previously been such a haven of peace – they had not impressed this teaching on their Miskito members who with their lack of formal education probably knew little or nothing about it. Nevertheless, opposition there has been by the Moravian Miskitos and this will continue until the Atlantic coast problem is solved.

There is no similarity or connection between the Miskitos and the Spanish-speaking evangelical pastors of CNPEN. There had however been a variety of incidents among fundamentalist Christians before CNPEN evolved in its present form. Some of these are referred to in a report on the Protestant churches in a 1982 edition of *Envio*.[13] The report refers first to problems with the Jehovah's Witnesses, which it correctly classifies as a sect rather than a Christian church. It goes on to note some of the attitudes attributed to various fundamentalist Protestant churches, examples being the public interpretation of the fierce floods of May 1982 as the judgment of God on the Sandinista government, and the preaching against participation in community activities and health campaigns organized by the Sandinista mass organizations. The *Envio* article refers also to the considerable involvement of US missionaries and institutions in the training of some fundamentalist-type pastors, and the very limited nature of some of that training. Quoting progressive Assemblies of God pastor Miguel Casco, the article says, 'In the majority of centres of biblical education, educative control was in the hands of North American missionaries who would ensure that the Nicaraguans received a strongly-influenced North American theology, which was boosted with anti-Communist, anti-Marxist material.'[14] The report goes on to comment on the troubled area near the northern border, describing how some fundamentalist and pentecostal churches appeared never to be harmed by *contras*. In some frontier areas Protestants left co-operatives after they were warned by the *contras* that 'co-operativism is opposed to religion'.

A further problem is illustrated by the *Comandante* of the Matagalpa region when he explains that some pastors and ministers have been objecting to members of the local militia attending worship in uniform, and even armed, because they were on duty. On other occasions troops who had been out on patrol, possibly for several days, have returned tired and perhaps wet from their duty, and the only place large enough to house them has been the village church. Some pastors accept these things, he says, but others do not.[15] Another source commented however that this negative reaction could be the result of fear, rather than any co-ordination by CNPEN. If pastors helped the Sandinistas they might be attacked, kidnapped or killed when the *contras* arrived. If they assisted the *contras* they could have problems with government authorities.

It is within CNPEN that specifically religious opposition has been focused and its leaders have demonstrated many ways of opposing the Sandinistas, including the type of ambiguous preaching described by Carlos Escorcia, warning members against joining the mass organizations or even expelling them for doing so, discouraging members from 'getting involved in politics' (i.e. supporting the government), and also maintaining and developing links with right-wing North American religious institutions. It was the last-mentioned activity which elicited a vigorous reaction in November 1985 when several pastors were detained by the security forces for periods ranging from a few hours to a few days, two of them having attended a seminar in California funded by conservative US church bodies.

One of the best-known of this group, Boanerges Mendoza, pastor of the First Pentecostal Church of Managua originally founded by the CAM of Dr Cyrus Scofield, is a former CNPEN President. Shortly after his initial brief detention he was visited by the US Embassy Secretary for Religious Affairs (a new post apparently created specially for Nicaragua) and following that was detained again by the security forces, this time for eleven days. Mendoza's church has a large membership of 600 and runs a sizeable school in its ancilliary premises. Perhaps as many as 220 church members now reside in the US however and he receives frequent invitations to preach and lecture in the USA. He claims not to receive any illegal US dollar support for his work (budgeted in January 1986 at four million *cordobas* a month, a fairly substantial sum) but explains that members of his church in the USA receive donations on his behalf, then members of their families still in Managua pay him the money.[16] This causes some concern to the government as Mendoza's church is influencing hundreds of people and school children in ways which may be damaging to the revolution. Mendoza himself claims to be a 'friend of the Sandinistas', and to be as critical of them to their faces as he is anywhere else. Sceptics however point to his very frequent US trips (twenty times in four years), his well-financed building programme and his close links with the US Embassy, where for example he is able to obtain visas for certain people within twenty-four hours.

The current President of CNPEN, International Baptist pastor Félix Rosales, claims that North American influence is minimal now in Nicaragua's evangelical churches, except perhaps for the Assemblies of God. He feels that the church was more free in Somoza's time because then 'the authorities were not always listening to what we say; we are faithful to the laws of this country, why can't they accept us? I would never for example preach against the SMP, this would be a wrong use of the pulpit.'[17] He claims that the government has very biased information about CNPEN because they get it from CEPAD. He also argues that there is much disaffection among the CEPAD membership, 'churches only continue to belong because of the resources CEPAD can provide'. Dr Parajón, CEPAD President, denies such charges, refers to the aggressive attitude CNPEN has adopted towards CEPAD and points to the evidence of links between CNPEN and the Institute of Religion and Democracy (IRD) which he feels may be using the CNPEN leadership, to some extent, for its own purposes.

The IRD was set up in the USA in 1981, apparently in response to the statement in the Santa Fe Report about the potential importance of the churches in Latin America in maintaining US dominance in the region. It received nearly half a million dollars in its first two years, mostly from right-wing foundations, and one of its specific targets has been the Sandinistas in Nicaragua. Given the philosophy of the IRD, if the CNPEN leaders did not exist the IRD would have had to invent them. As it is they, their statements and their experiences have been used, and blown up out of all proportion, to claim there is religious persecution in Nicaragua. Even Félix Rosales denies persecution, though he claims there is 'religious discrimination'. More will be said about the IRD's charges in the next chapter.

It does seem unlikely however that this small number of rather heterogeneous evangelical pastors are all willing agents of the CIA as has occasionally been suggested. They seem to be acting from three motivations: jealousy at the influence and ability of CEPAD and its leaders who have a much higher status with the government than they do; a genuinely conservative theology, which is still heavily North America-influenced, individualist, and believes that anything socialist is anti-Christian; and a desire to succumb to the careful wooing which has come from right-wing Christian circles in the US with their invitations to conferences, their roundabout financial assistance and their promises of a 'starring role' if ever the Sandinistas are overthrown. In short the Protestant opposition to *sandinismo* is almost pathetic, in that anything remotely discriminatory that it manages to bring upon itself is seized on by the US propaganda machine, and churned out in such a fashion that it can appear that the entire Protestant community of Nicaragua is about to suffer beatings, torture, or in selected cases the gas chambers. And this propaganda battle is one vital area of the wider ideological struggle to which we shall turn in the next chapter. Before that however we shall look fairly briefly at the activities of the *contras*, the US-sponsored opposition based in the neighbouring countries of Honduras and Costa Rica.

## *The Contras*

The counter-revolutionary opposition to the Sandinistas or *contras* (*contra* is Spanish for 'against') are the military wing of the Nicaraguan Democratic Force (FDN), the umbrella organization for the external political opposition to the Sandinistas. The *contras*' leadership is almost entirely made up of ex-members of Somoza's National Guard. Many of these fled to Honduras at the Sandinista victory in July 1979. Others were imprisoned for a time in Nicaragua, then released to lead a normal life in the community. A number of these remained in free Nicaragua, but a few decided to rejoin their former colleagues. The *contras* can offer food, shelter and a generous weekly dollar payment to the young men who are prepared to join them. The rank and file therefore come either from *campesino* youth who are attracted by cash and regular meals, or from pockets of communities in the north of the country from which Somoza recruited his Guard, and which therefore still have some family ties with the *contras*.

The FDN is variously estimated to have between 15,000 and 25,000 men under arms, depending on the flow of US money and equipment, and the state of the alliances with the Miskito fighters. The Miskitos tend to organize themselves separately from the FDN, though they still receive some of the North American largesse. The *contras* are based mostly in an area of Honduras which juts down into northern Nicaragua, and from which the local population of some 50,000 Hondurans have largely fled. Before 1985 there was also a fighting force based to the south in Costa Rica, under former Sandinista Eden Pastora, but the tenuous alliance between Pastora and the FDN finally broke in that year. Furthermore, the new Costa Rican government, elected in early 1986 has, despite US pressure, seemed unwilling to be used as a base for the Nicaraguan opposition.

The purpose of the *contras* appears quite simple: to create as much fear, disruption and destruction in the country as they can, particularly with respect to the Sandinista programmes in health, education, co-operatives and other development areas. Hence when communities are raided the *contras* attack teachers, health workers, community leaders, schools, clinics and community buildings. Many development workers have been injured, kidnapped or killed while undertaking their work of service to the people. CEPAD had to withdraw its programmes from a number of areas in the north after its people were murdered or kidnapped. Four CEPAD staff in the north-east were abducted in early 1985 and have not been heard from since.

The kidnapping, torture, rape and murder carried out by President Reagan's 'freedom fighters' have been described in detail in a report by the US Witness for Peace project and a book by Fr Teófilo Cabestrero, *Blood of the Innocent.* In his introduction Cabestrero writes:

> From 4 February to 20 February, 1985, I listened to testimony of some sixty persons, civilians in the north of Nicaragua, who had been the victims of kidnappings, bloody ambushes, rapes, and other kinds of assault by the *contras*, or who had survived the slaughter of their families or civilian friends.
>
> All of the accounts of the men and women I listened to, most of them poor, went straight into my note pad or my tape recorder and from there to these pages. I treated the words of these people with the sacred respect due the blood, death, grief, terror, desperation, and tears of the poor. The speakers are innocent, defenceless victims of a truly 'dirty war'. I was struck by the great detail with which the *campesinos*, who always spoke to me with grief and sometimes with terror and tears, remembered all these events, all the things that they themselves, their families, their co-operatives, or their communities had suffered. They recalled everything with minute exactness, even when they were telling me things that had happened two or three years before. And they knew the importance of an exact account. They knew that this was history. A survivor of a massacre near Wiwilí, a man whose whole being spoke of grief, told me, 'You see, I'm alive to tell the tale so that the world will know.'[18]

Cabestrero's book is a chronicle of obscenity, of a military force which claims to be engaged in a war against the anti-Christ, but itself exhibits all the signs of a total negation of Christianity. CEPAD's

*Pastoral Letter to the Peoples and Churches of the World* in July 1986 estimated that the *contra* war had led to 17,000 Nicaraguan deaths, 12,000 orphans, hundreds of widows, a quarter of a million people displaced and at least a billion dollars' worth of economic damage, including the destruction of bridges, schools, clinics, production facilities, leading to severe shortages of food, medicine, clothing and building materials. CEPAD's newsletters also report the latest *contra* atrocities. The June 1986 edition gave an account of the 4 May attack on Quiboto, a co-operative village in the Segovia mountains in the north, where 166 families who had fled from *contra* activities elsewhere had resettled. Twenty-one houses were burned, the co-operative's truck was destroyed and the store looted. The school was saved by a ten-year-old boy who put out the flames while under fire from the attackers. Six people were kidnapped, including a teacher, and have not been heard of since. In July CEPAD reported two similar attacks on co-operatives. In the first, eight people were killed, including three children, fifteen were wounded, and fourteen houses, three trucks, two full warehouses and the school destroyed. In the second, eighteen were killed and twenty-two injured. The August newsletter reported the blowing-up by a remote-control mine of a truck in which thirty-two people died: twelve women, twelve children and eight men. The lone survivor, pastor Nicolas Castilblanco of the United Pentecostal Mission, called the *contras* assassins who only knew how to kill *campesinos* and destroy their property. He asked the country's Catholic bishops to 'come and see how we suffer, come close to the people and realize what these criminals do'.[19] In October CEPAD reported on the assassination of a Baptist health promoter and his two brothers in Matagalpa province and in December gave a full account of the blowing up of a passenger truck near Pantasma where six were killed including a Nazarene deacon; a pentecostal pastor and his seven-year-old daughter each lost a leg.

The reaction of the Nicaraguan government to internal opposition, whether from Protestant pastors or the Catholic hierarchy must be seen within this context. The country is facing a brutal and vicious aggressor which in July 1986 received a further $110 million from the United States government. In December CEPAD reported that the day after President Reagan signed the Bill for the money 500 US Green Berets parachuted into Honduras and US naval vessels moved closer to the Atlantic coast. On 7 December planes bombed the villages of Wiwilí and Murra near the northern border killing several people.

Despite this pressure however the Sandinistas struggle to be fair, even to critics. On 31 October 1985, for example, a pastor named Matute was murdered in one of the northern areas. Two members of the Sandinista militia, who apparently thought Matute was a government opponent, were found to be responsible and arrested. After a trial at which CEPAD was specifically asked to send representatives they received maximum sentences of thirty years. There has been no Nicaraguan death penalty, even for convicted *contras*, since the revolution.

There are therefore many Christians who engage, wholeheartedly, with the revolutionary project in Nicaragua, and they are able to encourage, debate with and influence those with responsibility and power. There are also those who oppose it, and claim to do so from Christian motivation. Christians are instructed not to judge one another but it is certainly difficult not at least to raise questions about the nature of such motivation and the apparent political naïvety and theological illiteracy of its proponents.

# 5

# Struggling for Incarnation – The Theological Battleground

The very different perspectives on the Nicaraguan Revolution are clearly indicative of deeply conflicting beliefs. At the root of what is happening in both the Protestant and the Catholic churches is a profound struggle in ideology and indeed in theology. This struggle has important implications, not only for the revolutionary process but also for the whole world. An analytical paper, which I shall look at in more detail in the third section of this chapter, offers the view that although in 1979 the revolution took military and political power, and economic power too to some extent, 'the structures of ideological power remain almost intact, even deprived of the social framework which sustained them'.[1]

In this chapter I shall explore the different forms which the ideological and theological struggle takes within Catholicism as well as within Protestantism, in the hope of making a contribution to mutual understanding. I shall also explore the ideological implications of the pressures brought to bear on both Catholics and Protestants by the right-wing US religious and political forces.

There seem to be four main problem areas for Protestantism – biblicism, other-worldism, North Americanism and a pacifism which relates to both the military and the political spheres. Underlying the particular manifestations of theological conflict, however, there appears to be a fundamental disagreement about the meaning of the Incarnation. Perhaps the differences are so deep and so profound that all the factions cannot be right, and not everyone can legitimately continue to claim to be Christian. Before I attempt to give an account of the theological debate I would like to set it in the context of what the Sandinistas themselves have said and done about religion.

### *The Sandinista View of Religion*

It might be expected that given the active participation of many Christians in the revolutionary struggle the Sandinistas would have a rather different perspective on religion from that of other similar movements further back in history. Indeed I have already mentioned that there are reckoned to be three main streams of thought combining in the Nicaraguan Revolution, *sandinismo* (the thought of General Sandino and his followers), Marxist-Leninism and Christianity. There are particularly important links between the first and last of these. As we saw earlier Sandino felt strongly that he had divine support for his cause. The chief founder of the new Sandinista movement, Carlos Fonseca, studied theology and at one time was contemplating being a Catholic priest. Most Sandinistas therefore feel particularly aggrieved when one of the main criticisms of their revolution is that it is anti-religious, although at the same time there are a number of hard-line Marxist-Leninists in the FSLN who do believe religion should be actively discouraged.

The Sandinistas made an initial statement on the freedom of religion in October 1979, and followed it up with a fuller one on 7 October 1980 which is reproduced in Appendix 5. It begins with a complaint about a 'pernicious campaign of misinterpretation and lies' and the attempts to 'sow confusion' by suggestions that 'the FSLN is making use of religion at this time with the idea of suppressing it later on'. The statement points out that many 'patriotic revolutionary Christians' are involved in the FSLN and the government and goes on to describe how the motivation of such people is their faith, and how in some cases this has inspired people to die for the cause. It recounts how other Christians, even in the leadership of the churches, bravely denounced the persecution of Somoza and for this they were harassed, attacked, exiled and even murdered. 'Thus Christians have been an integral part of our revolutionary history . . . This opens new and interesting possibilities for Christian participation in the revolutions of other lands.'[2]

The statement goes on to declare the freedom to hold any religious faith, or none, in the new Nicaragua. It then refers to the Marxist view that religion can be a tool for the alienation of the people and for class exploitation, but notes that when Christians 'standing on their faith' respond to the needs of people and of history, 'their beliefs drive them to revolutionary activity'. Christians may therefore become members of the FSLN. The statement refers later to divisions in the churches, and says that these are a matter for Christians, not for the government. The statement expresses the hope that priest *compañeros* who are active in government will continue to serve the revolution in this way, but recognizes that a person may wish to withdraw for personal reasons 'and that too is his right'. It is a statement without precedent in the modern era of revolutionary movements.

The participation in government by both Protestant and Catholic Christians has already been referred to. It may be appropriate just to mention again the Catholic priests holding high office, as it is around their participation that much controversy has flared in church circles. Fr Miguel d'Escoto, a priest of the US Maryknoll Order, has been Foreign Minister in Nicaragua since the revolution. Fr Ernesto Cardenal, the priest-poet who founded the Solentiname Community, has been Minister of Culture since 1979. His brother Fr Fernando Cardenal was originally responsible for the National Literacy Crusade and in 1984 became Minister of Education. He was expelled from the Jesuit Order at the end of 1984. Fr Edgar Parrales has also served in the government and became the Nicaraguan Ambassador to the United Nations. He decided to resign the priesthood in 1985 but his request has not so far been accepted. There are other priests such as Fr Xavier Gorostiaga who hold or have held key government posts. All those of ministerial rank within the government have been denied the right to exercise their priestly ministry by the Vatican. The Cardenal brothers and Miguel d'Escoto tell their stories in *Ministers of God, Ministers of the People.*[3]

## *The Catholic Church*

Although this book is about the Protestant churches, because Catholicism is clearly the majority denomination in Nicaragua it is necessary for theological purposes to be aware of the kind of tensions which have developed between the government and some of the Catholic hierarchy. Catholics in Nicaragua are anxious to make it clear that it is mainly Cardinal Obando y Bravo and some of his episcopal colleagues who are anti-Sandinista but the majority of the church follows what the cardinal says and if he were to reverse his position and support the government almost all of them would dutifully follow. Some of the bishops however are less than happy with the views held by the cardinal; this becomes clear when some Catholic statements and the way they are issued is examined carefully.

The cardinal and his supporters have cited several cases of what they regard as persecution. This includes being forced to pay more to the teachers in their schools (and then being offered government money to pay the difference), the expulsion in 1985 of ten foreign priests, the seizing of the first edition of their new magazine *Iglesia* (Church) in the autumn of 1985 because they refused to comply with the law of registration, and the removal from the air in early 1986 of the Catholic radio station, after several disputes with the authorities including failure to broadcast a legally-required government statement because of a 'technical oversight'. Part of the government's extreme irritation with Obando is his refusal to condemn the violence of the *contras*, while continuing to criticize the defence policies of the Sandinistas and urge them to dialogue with the FDN. This argument reached a climax in mid-1986 when the cardinal's spokesman Fr Bismarck Carballo was refused permission to re-enter the country after a tour of Europe in which he had persistently criticized the government. This was immediately followed by the expulsion of one of the senior bishops, Bishop Vega, for speaking in apparent support of *contra* violence. The day after Vega's press conference the incident to which I referred in the previous chapter took place: a remote-control mine blew up a lorry and thirty-two people were killed. CEPAD leaders expressed their concern about the government's treatment of the two clergymen but the newly-elected Superintendent of the Church of the Nazarene in Nicaragua supported the government decision and stated, 'Bishop Vega was not acting as a pastor but as an internal agent of the counter-revolution.'[4] At his next homily after the expulsions the cardinal said that Carballo and Vega 'bore the mark of Christ' but made no reported reference to the thirty-two murdered *campesinos*.

There is clearly a fundamental difference of opinion between supporters of the Sandinistas and some of the Catholic hierarchy over what has been going on in the country and what the right response of Christians should be. What are the reasons for those around Obando adopting the position they have? In my view this cannot really be understood without reference to the policies of the United States. Suffice it to say that casting round in the early eighties for a viable internal opposition to the Sandinistas the State Department apparently fastened on the archbishop as one of the few available candidates. Then in 1983, somewhat surprisingly in view of his qualifications but not so surprisingly in view of the close correlation of world-view between the US Government and Pope John Paul II's Vatican, the archbishop became the Central American Cardinal. Local observers thought that at least three of the five local archbishops were better equipped. Leaders in other denominations have their own views on the hierarchy's motivations. When asked what he thought was the basis of the problems between the cardinal and the Sandinistas a senior Anglican, after some thought, said, 'It is at root a struggle for power. The Catholic church has been powerful in Nicaragua since the Spanish came. It felt put out after the revolution and determined to regain its influence. The cardinal manipulates the religious beliefs of the poor people, he uses one of Managua's largest churches with the most famous icon to make his public announcements. It hurts me to see the faith of humble people used in that way.'[5]

A Catholic priest in the north of the country, who suffered torture before 1979 for his support of the revolutionary struggle, remarked, 'The bishops have a false sense of reality. They expect the revolution to fail so they can re-establish "the true church". But it won't happen.

The people will continue to support the revolution indefinitely. Many of the young people are prepared to die.'[6] Indeed many Catholics who support the Sandinistas are desperately afraid that the cardinal's attitudes will drive many away from the churches, especially among the young. However, a faltering dialogue was formally resumed between the Sandinistas and the Catholic leadership in late 1986.

### *A Sociological Analysis*

In 1982 the Nicaraguans held a Social Science Congress at which there was a presentation on the religious question by Miguel Casco, President of CEPRES, Assemblies of God pastor and associate of the Antonio Valdivieso Centre.[7] This presentation focused on what Casco called the sects, which he defined as including a large proportion of the smaller evangelical and fundamentalist churches, some of which are also CEPAD members. CEPAD however describes those churches which are its members as denominations and those which are not as sects. Terminology is certainly difficult in this field; it is not easy to regard a group of Christians with two or three churches which have split off from a larger body as a new denomination. Perhaps CEPAD's terminology is the most useful for us, but we should be aware that CEPAD would treat as denominations some of Casco's sects.

Casco points out in his paper 'The Sects in Nicaragua: Heritage of the Past and Instruments of Imperialism', that the ideological struggle in the religious field is not an accident: 'It is initiatied by groups who will never win the hearts of the people and so use religion, particularly the sects, as a platform for destabilization.' Those who have brought about this struggle 'are not interested in the practice of the faith but they do it because of their links with the counter-revolution'.[8] The enemies of the revolution, knowing that Nicaraguans are a religious people, are trying to persuade them they are struggling for the faith, against atheistic Communism. These people and their backers, says Casco, see that if Christians become an integral part of the revolution this will make the whole Latin American revolution indestructible. So the enemies seek to conceal 'a counter-political strategy beneath a religious cloak'. This observation is supported by many of the victims of *contra* activity where those escaping from kidnaps frequently describe the *contras* as claiming religious motivation for fighting what they describe as a 'holy war'.[9]

The original Protestant expansion into South America during the nineteenth century was also a cultural one, Casco says, with capitalist and colonialist dimensions. The US missionaries allowed Protestantism to be identified with liberalism: anti-Catholic, anti-ecumenical, apolitical, other-worldly. The identification was emphasized in Nicaragua when the Somoza family came to power in the 1920s. Somoza gave political and economic freedom to North American missionaries who consciously or unconsciously made a great contribution to cementing the ideological bases of imperialism in the Protestant churches. Ruiz and Sullivan voice this view in their paper on the history of Protestantism. 'We believe the Protestant churches of Nicaragua are a result of the US missionary project during the stage of the imperialist expansion of the capitalist system, it being allied, consciously or unconsciously, to neo-colonialism; our faith came filtered through the perspective of liberal capitalism.'[10]

In Casco's opinion it was no mistake that the evangelical churches were encouraged to penetrate to the mountains of the Matagalpa region in the first years of Somoza's rule. This was where Sandino had had his main base. The penetration was a North American project to obtain sympathy and loyalty for Somoza in the northern mountains and legitimize his power. When the Cuban Revolution took place in 1959 the area was flooded with anti-Communist teaching, including propaganda statements about the Cubans forcing Christians to give up their faith. Casco believes the sects have been encouraged in order to manipulate religious thinking, to push it back from social and political concerns, to see the crisis as cultural and moral instead. There are people who use religion to serve the interests of the counter-revolution, and to convince innocent believers. Now, says Casco, 'sectors of the economically dominant classes who have never before declared themselves followers of Jesus Christ and lovers of the gospel' are using religious belief to help them put together a political platform which will help them regain power. The sects have adopted a 'theology of death'. 'We believe that the theology of death, as part of the dominant ideology in our region, feeds on anti-life projects and is incarnated in projects of injustice and shame. At the same time this theology constitutes part of imperialism's plan and it is for this that the sects are being converted as reproducers of the theology of the dominant class.'[11] The concept of 'the theology of death' is one to which we shall return.

## *The United States Project*

For a tiny, weak and impoverished country, Nicaragua has taken up an enormous amount of the time and energy of the US authorities. Do they really believe that Nicaragua is 'a threat to the security of the United States' as President Reagan has frequently stated? The background of the Monroe doctrine, the US view of Latin America as its sphere of influence and more recently the Rockefeller initiative in 1969 and the Santa Fe Report of 1980, have been referred to already. The root ideological problem for the US seems to lie in its deep anti-Communism and its great suspicion of Soviet motives especially in any political changes taking place close to its own borders. The US government issues a constant stream of documents, reports and statements on the situation in Central America, constantly accusing the Sandinistas of bad faith, military subversion and subjection to Cuba and the Soviet Union.

In December 1985 General Vernon Walters in a speech at the United Nations stated that the 'Sandinistas have accelerated their efforts to consolidate a totalitarian régime along the Cuban model. They are moving to silence internal dissent and to increase military pressure against the democratic resistance with the assistance of new shipments of Soviet arms.' He went on to claim that the suspension of civil liberties in October 1985 had been 'to neutralize the internal democratic opposition' and that the Catholic church had been a particular target. According to Walters, church leaders had been interrogated, threatened and warned that foreign priests 'will be expelled if Sandinista orders are disobeyed'.[12] In February 1986 the US Information Service published a statement accusing the Sandinistas of secret agreements with the Soviet Union and a massive military build up, including widespread conscription. It went on 'in efforts to enforce the draft the government raids schools and cinemas, and conscripts seminarians'.[13] Nicaraguan Christians, commenting on the last of these accusations, noted that it had been demonstrated that some young men had sought to enter the Catholic priesthood simply to escape military service. The following month the State Department issued a report *In Their Own Words (Testimony of Nicaraguan Exiles)* which told the stories of nine people who had fled Nicaragua for various reasons between 1979 and 1985. Among them was a Moravian pastor, victim of the conflict between the Sandinistas and the Miskitos in the Rio Coco area in 1980. Another, pentecostal pastor Prudencio Baltodano, seemed to have fallen victim to the deep suspicion of some of the Sandinista military towards the independent churches. The highest-ranking escapée was the former Vice-Minister of Justice. The report concludes by claiming that the Nicaraguan Revolution has failed most to help those it was supposed to be for, though makes no mention of the part played in any failure by the economic boycott or the US-backed *contra* war.

The message of militarism and the Cuban and Soviet domination of Nicaragua is also the theme of a glossy report by the US State and Defence Departments published in June 1986. Entitled *The Challenge to Democracy in Central America*, the section on Nicaragua is called *Marxism and Militarism*. On its first page it pictures President Ortega alongside Fidel Castro over a text, 'Fidel Castro with his long-time colleague Daniel Ortega . . . Castro started supplying the Sandinistas with weapons in the early 1960s and intensified the clandestine flow of arms in 1979.' Other pictures in the section include Soviet-made military helicopters, which it is alleged are flown by Cuban pilots 'against the democratic resistance' and Soviet T-55 tanks which are 'an intimidating weapon to Nicaragua's neighbours and the Nicaraguan people'. The text fails to point out that the terrain where the 'democratic resistance' is being fought is totally unsuitable for use by tanks. The Nicaraguans are also accused of having the largest army in the region, and of assisting subversion in neighbouring countries, particularly El Salvador. There is no reference to the United States' own activities in Central American countries. The section concludes with the assertion that 'in several new prisons' constructed by the Sandinistas they are using techniques 'Josef Stalin used in 1930s to convince visitors to the Soviet Union of the "humane" nature of the Soviet penal system'.[14]

The US government is understandably reluctant for there to be too much public debate over the International Court of Justice decision in the Hague in July 1986 which found the United States guilty of supporting activities designed to destabilize and undermine the government of Nicaragua. Despite the fact that it had been the main proponent and founder of the World Court in 1920 and despite its great irritation when in 1979 Iran refused to accept the Court's jurisdiction when its students occupied the US Embassy in Tehran, in 1985 the US itself failed to offer any defence against Nicaragua's charges, and then refused to accept the Court's decision. International lawyers have noted that such an attitude on the part of a major world power represents a contempt for international law which makes the world a more dangerous place. The British government supported the US by abstaining on a United Nations resolution in late October seeking a response to the World Court decision, under the UN Charter. Calling Nicaragua presumptuous for seeking a 'selective application' of the Charter, the British UN representative said, 'We are unable to support a resolution which fails . . . to acknowledge that Nicaragua has largely brought its troubles upon itself.' The British government takes a similar position over aid, contributing only £800,000 in 1985/6, largely in co-financing with voluntary agencies, compared with £9 million contributed by Sweden.

Later in 1986 the US government was thrown on the defensive in its Nicaraguan policy by two events. The first was the shooting down on 5 October of the C-123 plane in which two US citizens were killed and one – Eugene Hasenfus – captured. The second was the revelation that the *contras* had continued to receive funding through sales of arms to Iran during the period when Congress had officially suspended its support. The C-123, flying arms to the *contras* from the main civil and military airport in El Salvador, was clearly an example of the sort of operation in which the CIA specializes when carrying out activities not sanctioned by Congress. Although sentenced to thirty years' imprisonment, Hasenfus was pardoned in time for Christmas 1986, an act which cannot have been popular in Nicaragua, in view of the thousands killed by US-sponsored military action between 1981 and 1986. The disclosure of the operation in which missiles had been sold to Iran to assist in the release of US hostages in Lebanon, and payments made via Israel had been transferred from a Swiss bank account to fund the *contras*, provided an extreme example of the style in which US foreign policy is sometimes conducted. With evidence pointing to the complicity of both Vice-President Bush and President Reagan in the secret *contra* funding, the Presidency rocked dangerously in the closing weeks of 1986. 'Irangate' had begun.

In its efforts to divert accusations the US administration sought to identify what the USSR was said to be doing in Afghanistan with what it was doing in Nicaragua. One of the US delegation leaders at a security conference in Europe, Ambassador Robert Frowick, said on 2 December, 'In both cases, the Soviet Union is attempting forcibly to help place in power a totalitarian political leadership which is opposed by the masses of the people.' Responsibility for the current overall crisis in Central America 'lies squarely on the shoulders of the Sandinistas' Frowick charged. They have waged 'a campaign of systematic repression at home and subversion against all their neighbours'.[15] In a letter to me the same month the US Embassy claimed, 'Support for the democratic resistance (i.e. *the contras*) is an essential element of our effort to achieve a negotiated solution. We continue to believe that the aid to the resistance forces is a vital element to prevent the consolidation of a Communist régime in Nicaragua.'[16]

In the context of a certain amount of US paranoia it is perhaps important to remember that the population of the extremely poor and under-developed country of Nicaragua is not much more than three million – a little over 1% of that of the United States, and therefore may not represent quite as large a threat as some North American politicians seem to think.

Let us turn now from an overall perspective of US policies to the narrower confines of the religious sector.

I have referred elsewhere to the adoption of the Catholic hierarchy, the links with Pentecostal pastors, the charges of religious persecution, and the funding for every kind of opposition (from the opposition press to the *contra* army) which has come from US sources. But who are the main actors in the religious sphere? We have referred earlier to the Institute for Religion and Democracy (IRD). The IRD was highlighted in a book published in 1984 by Ana Maria Ezcurra *The Vatican and the Reagan Administration*.[17] She believes that the IRD has tried to build contacts with both the evangelical churches and the Catholic hierarchy, and is very close to the Reagan administration's policies, being willing even to support military intervention. The Institute appears to regard everything critical of free enterprise as 'totalitarian' and a creature of Soviet Marxist-Leninism. It has described liberation theology as Marxist and tried to label all progressive Catholics as the 'popular church', and thereby distinguish them from the 'official' Catholic church. The IRD has even claimed that Nicaraguan State Security has recruited Christians of the 'popular church' to be its agents within Catholicism.

According to Ezcurra the IRD fastened on the conflict between the Sandinistas and the Miskitos as a major opportunity for attack, and developed strong links with the leadership of Misurasata, one of the Miskito organizations. It made claims that Sandinista aggression had caused thousands of Indians to flee, and said that government forces were trying to assassinate the Catholic Bishop of Bluefields, Mgr Schaeffer, when he left the country in December 1983 with some exiles. The IRD cast doubt on the validity of the 1984 elections in Nicaragua, implying they were fraudulent and undemocratic. Ezcurra gives details of the IRD's criticisms of progressive North American Christians as well as its criticisms of the US National Council of Churches and the World Council of Churches. There are far too many similarities between Reaganite policies and IRD activities for these to be coincidence.

The heavily-funded IRD also has links with some of the supposedly Christian organizations which have been funding and pleading the *contra* cause in the United States. In a detailed article 'In the Name of Relief' in the *Sojourners* magazine, Vicki Kemper listed nearly a dozen such organizations, for example Operation Blessing, the World Anti-Communist League, the Nicaraguan Refugee Fund (NRF) and the Christian Broadcasting Network (CBN).[18] According to Kemper these groups have raised millions of dollars mostly in 'humanitarian aid'. The effect of this aid on Nicaragua, however, is to attract workers off the land, who then become refugees and provide a source of recruitment for the *contras*. It was in fact the CIA who began the first fund-raising for the *contras*, through the Human Development Foundation, which channelled money to the Nicaraguan Refugee Fund. The CIA co-operated with the National Democratic Force, the co-ordinating *contra* agency, to develop the NRF. But it has been the Christian Broadcasting Network of Rev. Pat Robertson which has provided a religious platform for North American anti-Sandinista views. It has been Robertson too, through his television and radio programmes, who has sought to put political pressure on the administration. On his '700 Club' programme in April 1985 Robertson said, 'I want us to pray about the vote in Congress because this is a very important vote, and the craven submission of our leaders and Congress to the demands of Communism makes you sick to your stomach . . . We want to pray that God will somehow speak to these people. Why don't we pray that the Lord will give aid to those who are struggling against Communist rule?'[19]

Lending support to Casco's view, which I referred to in the previous section, a NACLA (North American Congress on Latin America) report of 1984 entitled *The Salvation Brokers: Conservative Evangelicals in Central America* notes the considerable spread of evangelicalism in Latin America and the enormous amount of financial support coming from North America. Worldwide 'in 1979 there were more than 53,500 US and Canadian overseas missionaries working with agencies which grossed nearly $1.2 billion in income . . . approximately 1,500 North American missionaries were working in Central America'.[20] What is more, 'the kind of evangelical Protestantism which is sweeping Central America removes its adherents from social struggle and reform, places the onus on God rather than human beings to act, and results in submissive resignation while waiting for Jesus' return to bring about change'.[21] The report focuses on the role of the Central American Mission in this process and lists some of the US big business executives and corporations who support these missionary enterprises. It also draws attention to the co-ordinating role of Latin American Missions (LAM), which although making reference in its programmes to the problems of poverty and the need for social justice is also very strongly anti-Communist. NACLA details the work of the Campus Crusade for Christ founded by a Presbyterian lay-person, with its conservative theology. It is directed towards students and points them firmly away from involvement in the world. CCC has a global budget of $90 million and aims to show its propaganda film *Jesus* to 'two to three billion people in this decade'.[22]

The report lists a number of examples from the early 1980s in which fundamentalist churches sought to undermine the infant Sandinista régime, using radio programmes, anti-government preaching and criticism of government projects to demonstrate their opposition. It quotes examples of financial incentives to evangelical pastors, describing how each month one pastor 'divides up 375,000 *cordobas* into eighteen sealed envelopes each destined for a denominational contact who will share out the "salary support" among a carefully-screened list of pastors . . . Six hundred pastors – about 40% of all the 1,500 active in Nicaragua – participate in this "salary support programme". They receive a . . . 50% boost to their salaries.'[23]

The wide variety of examples I have given indicates the extent of US pressure on the Sandinistas, using the religious dimension as one important part of the battle-ground. What is the final intention of the US? Does President Reagan want to intimidate the Sandinistas? Or does he want to destroy them? The view of senior officials at the US Embassy is that Nicaragua is a victim of the Soviet tactic of changing governments by subversive means and that strategically the USSR is interested in airfields and ports close to the USA and the Panama Canal. They claim that the Sandinistas have made 'secret speeches' in which all nine of the *Comandantes* have declared they are aiming for another Cuba, taking control first of military and state security, then government, then the economy and the unions, and so on. They will save the churches till last, as being the most difficult to control! Embassy spokespersons have pointed to the controls on business, the churches and the media as denials of human rights, but asserted that the US economic boycott is not having a negative effect on the Nicaraguan people, nor driving ordinary Nicaraguans towards the Soviet Union. The US demand has been for an end to Sandinista support for the other guerrilla movements (which they deny anyway), severance of Nicaraguan military ties with Cuba and the Soviet bloc, a reduction of military strength, and the fulfilment of democratic pluralism (by which the US is understood to mean the election of its chosen Presidential candidate Arturo Cruz). When a US citizen on hearing a senior Embassy official list these requirements murmured, 'You mean, you want them to say "Uncle",' the official had the grace to blush.[24]

Those most closely associated with the Nicaraguan government, both in the churches and outside, believe that certainly in some departments of the Reagan administration, and even in the mind of the President himself, there is a determination to destroy the Sandinistas. They say that despite all the attempts at mediation, such as the Contadora process which involved mediation by other Latin American countries, and all efforts to find a compromise, the US is fundamentally opposed to the continuation of a government in Central America which it cannot control. It is *The Threat of a Good Example*[25] which might encourage others in Central and Latin America to do the same, which the US cannot countenance. According to this perspective the only considerations which have prevented the US invading so far are the increasingly efficient Sandinista armed forces and local people's militias, who would undoubtedly inflict considerable losses on the US Army – and then retreat to the mountains to continue guerrilla warfare – and the strength of international opinion, which is not at all persuaded that a military invasion could be justified, although the British government in particular has failed to voice any strong objections. Nicaragua represents the possibility that a small and poor country can detach itself, at least partially, from the international capitalist economy and succeed in feeding, clothing, educating and sheltering its people better than before. The United States cannot afford to see that happen, and appears willing to prevent it by any means it can. That is why the churches are part of the ideological battleground in this 'David and Goliath' confrontation.

## *The Theological Encounter*

I outlined the ground of the theological struggle at the beginning of this chapter: biblicism, other-worldism, North Americanism and a false pacifism. The term 'biblicism' refers to the belief of many Christians that they should read the Bible as if it had indeed been delivered on tablets of stone, as if it related entirely to events of two thousand years ago and more, and as if it does not relate in any effective way to the events of today. Putting it simply, to one group of Christians the Exodus is an account of how God liberated some hundreds of thousands of Hebrew slaves from Egypt into the Promised Land on a certain occasion about three and a half thousand years ago, with no particular implications for today; to another group it is a story which encapsulates the truth that God is always seeking to lead his people out of slavery and into a 'promised land' and that he will be deeply involved in every age and place where slaves and oppressed peoples are struggling for liberation. The first group often, though not always, treat the Bible in a fundamentalist and deeply limiting fashion; certainly this seems to be the case among some of the strongly evangelical and pentecostal churches and sects in Nicaragua.

Such a view of the Bible goes hand-in-hand with 'other-worldism' which treats this world as a sinful and undesirable place, in which the believer must not get too involved, in case he or she should become stained and sullied by its wickedness. Political activity is by definition concerned with the affairs of the world and therefore in certain Christian circles in Nicaragua to speak of the needs of the poor, or solidarity with the oppressed or with the revolution, is political and therefore not the business of Christianity. This can lead to a dualism in which there may be political involvement by a believer, or even a pastor, outside the church, but such concerns must not be brought inside. 'Other-worldism' leads to a shutting of eyes and ears to the needs of humanity and results in a wilful ignorance about such needs, and accusations of Communism against those who seek to respond to them.

'North Americanism' is tied profoundly to the manner in which Protestant Christianity came to Central America. It arrived clothed in all the cultural expectations and aspirations of triumphal western capitalism, cocksure of the ability of white Anglo-Saxon Protestants to solve the problems of the world. Such an approach leads to a destruction of the receiving people's culture and identity, to the domination of decision-making, to organizations like the Society for the American Way of Life in Nicaragua and to the conviction that God really is made in the image of a powerful, white, male citizen of the United States. North Americanism is individualistic: it is the personal and not the collective soul that must be saved. North Americanism produces economic dependence, sometimes simply of the local churches, sometimes of the entire nation. Anything Communist or even socialist is to be regarded as evil. Anything which denies the all-importance of the individual and suggests a more communitarian approach to human need or to salvation is to be regarded as more or less of the devil. In this world-view those who do not reach the required individual achievement-level are irrelevant and superfluous.

Then there is 'pacifism', a pacifism which in Nicaragua operates in both military and political dimensions. In the military, the term 'pacifists' refers to those who criticize the SMP. For there are churches which have suddenly remembered that there is biblical teaching against violence, and that Jesus' teaching can be read as being opposed to military activity. Supporters of the Sandinistas in Nicaragua point rather indignantly to the very recent discovery of this aspect of Christian teaching by some fundamentalist churches. Nothing was heard of Christian pacifism or conscientious objection in the Somoza era, they say, and no attempts were made to oppose recruitment to the National Guard. The debate is reminiscent of those between European Christians, who, forgetting their support for the Allies in 1939–45, suddenly became pacifists when African liberation movements, after decades of non-violence, reluctantly adopted armed struggle and asked for support.

Political pacifism involves objection to class struggle, a position which is also being increasingly advocated by the Vatican. Injustice and inequality in society may not be consistent with the Christian ideal according to political pacifists, but it is regarded as wholly unacceptable to analyse the causes in terms of class structures of domination, and then seek to do something about their abolition. There is strong resistance to the proposition by radical Christians that as long as these structures remain they will continue to prevent the poor from obtaining their rightful place in the community.

It is this kind of theology, biblicist, other-worldly, falsely pacifist, and ideologically and economically captive to the USA, which some progressive Christians in Latin America have described as 'a theology of death'. They have employed this term because it ultimately involves external control, dependency, structural injustice and despair, and leads to a state of mind and being which looks for salvation only outwards to an external god who is remarkably North American in character. This deity is removed from the world, possesses almighty power, observes and considers, has decided when to intervene and will at some point do so. When he does it will be to transport the faithful into the new age and cast the unbelievers (especially atheistic Communists) into outer darkness for ever. In the case of the Catholic hierarchy there may be a gloss on this, in which God will intervene earlier, to first restore the Catholic church to its former glory as the second power of the nation (if not the first). The theology of death is the opposite of liberation theology, which encourages the oppressed first to analyse and understand their situation, and then to act to change it. Here the liberating God is a personally involved and committed God, who suffers with his people, and struggles with them, along the way of the Cross, to a new life of resurrection. These two views of God, deliberately caricatured here, represent a fundamental difference, and cause clear polarization, within both Protestant and Catholic churches. It is a polarization which strikes deep into church, community and even family life. Is this phenomenon confined just to Nicaragua? 'No,' says one knowledgeable observer of the Central American churches, 'It is just that it has been allowed to surface here. You will find the same deep divisions among Christians in other countries in the region, it is just that in those countries there is little freedom to express them.'[26]

Ultimately these two positions represent profoundly different understandings of the meaning of the Incarnation, one of the basic Christian doctrines. Did Jesus come to earth on just one occasion to demonstrate that this distant God, this God-outside-the-world, loves humanity? Did he come to show that this God cares so much that he would offer his own son to be crucified and then magically raise him from the dead so that each human being who believes in him may be saved? Does he intend to return at some future time in order to draw those who have been saved to himself, casting the others into eternal darkness? Or is Jesus the key participator in God's on-going involvement in the painful human struggle against selfishness and sin? Does he show that God wants humanity to be a loving, caring community which can grow away from the sin and fear that crucified Jesus? Does he demonstrate that such a community involves living together, in something at least approaching justice, peace and freedom, a life 'in the kingdom' which continues, even through and in spite of death? This is of course the view that the progressive Protestant Christians of Nicaragua have adopted, and which they are seeking to express, alongside many fellow Catholic believers and indeed some non-believers or agnostics within the Sandinista movement. It is in these perceptions of Christ that we see most profoundly the polarization of the faith in the Nicaraguan situation.

## *The Evangelical Insurrection*

A new dimension which has been opened up in Nicaragua is a movement which has been labelled the Evangelical Insurrection, conceived by Fr Miguel d'Escoto, the Maryknoll priest who has been Foreign Minister of Nicaragua since 1979. ('Evangelical' here of course refers to the real good news rather than conservative forms of belief.) Between mid-1985 and mid-1986 the Insurrection took the form of three initiatives – a month-long fast by Fr d'Escoto in

July 1985, a series of meetings and rallies for peace the following September with visiting theologians and Christian activists, and the *via crucis* pilgrimage for Lent 1986.

Fr d'Escoto explained his concept of the Evangelical Insurrection in a long interview in July 1985, shortly before his fast.[27] He spoke of how the Nicaraguan people are successfully resisting US aggression on four battlefields: military, economic, diplomatic, and legal. First, the *contra* army has been contained. 'The only way left is . . . to use US troops,' says d'Escoto. Second, despite all the US boycott can do 'our economy continues to survive', although in the diplomatic arena he admits that political pressures on friendly governments have had some success. Lastly, with reference to the legal battleground Fr d'Escoto said, 'I am 100% sure that we will win the decision of the World Court.' (As we mentioned in the previous section of this chapter, Nicaragua was suing for damages against the US government and won the case in July 1986.) Hence,

> Reagan needs to create internal conditions in the US to launch an invasion, and it is clear he has advanced a long way in achieving this goal . . . In the remaining gap are the people of the United States. They are the ones who can and should stop Reagan. To achieve this the most effective actions are those of thousands of women and men who have made a Pledge of Resistance against the aggressiveness of US government leaders.[28]

D'Escoto goes on to speak of the need to be creative and audacious in the efforts to stop the Reagan administration carrying out its threats and plans. After the four 'fronts' already named, he says, 'It is time to move into a fifth one, "the theological arena". Those of us who are Christians ought to be in this area, and there defeat Reagan. He has been using . . . "theological arguments" to persuade the US public. And this presentation of the conflict will become more acute: he, the United States, American civilization, represent "good". In Nicaragua there is "evil", terrorism, which must be annihilated.'[29] D'Escoto rejects however the temptation to produce many documents of denunciation. 'The world is inundated with documents. Action is what is missing. We must do something. I have thought, therefore, it is up to us as Christians to develop non-violent actions which vividly express what cannot be said on paper.' He continues, 'I saw clearly before God that it was I, as Foreign Minister and priest, who must be the first to do something, and to do it now. That is why I decided to fast.' In the same interview d'Escoto tells how two experiences of faith have been maturing in his life as a Christian and a priest, the mystery of the Cross and the un-Christian nature of violence.

> The Christian ideal is a non-violent ideal, it is a project of non-violence. In Nicaragua, we Christians should incorporate non-violent methods into our legitimate military defence. I always think of Martin Luther King . . . for me he is without a doubt the greatest saint of our times. We Christians are countering aggressive violence with legitimate defence, but we also have the responsibility to make creative non-violence a key element of the Good News that we proclaim and practise daily.[30]

An example of such creative non-violence was the *via crucis* – the March for Peace and Life – to the capital Managua from Jalapa, a town in the northern border region where the US-backed *contras* are continually causing disruption and death. The march took place in Lent 1986, covering a distance of some 320 kilometres (200 miles). The journey took a fortnight, spent on the hot, dusty roads of Nicaragua, stopping in villages and towns along the way for prayers, worship, meals and rest. Local communities provided the necessary food and accommodation. The marchers varied from a core group of some sixty who completed the whole distance, to several hundreds as the procession reached and left sizeable towns. Each day represented one of the fourteen Stations of the Cross, and began with suitable prayer and meditation. A high point came when the march reached Estelí, a town famous for its vigorous resistance in the final weeks of Somoza's struggle to remain in power. Here the fourteen Stations of the Cross were undertaken in one long procession around the town under torchlight, and completed with a service in front of the Cathedral in which thousands took part. The *via crucis* finally ended with a great mass in the old Cathedral Square in Managua, after a triumphal but dignified procession into the city along the north highway, under the baking sun. About sixty priests from several countries participated, including two or three Protestants, and the worship conducted by the light of torches included music from the *Misa Campesina* (the Peasant Mass) and contributions from some of those who walked the *via crucis*. The torches used at the times of evening worship have become symbols of the Evangelical Insurrection.

In an interview shortly before the *via crucis* Fr d'Escoto referred with some heat to the deaths of over 15,000 Nicaraguans since the 1979 Revolution, which is proportionately three times as many as the North American deaths during the Second World War. 'As many of our people have been displaced as would be equivalent to the population of New York State.' He believes that the United States is suffering from the arrogance of power. 'They expect us to worship them because they are who they are.'[31] He made it crystal clear however that many Nicaraguan Christians will continue to resist US aggression, some non-violently, some in the defence forces, but in many cases if necessary with their lives.

Until the *via crucis* the Evangelical Insurrection had been largely confined to Catholics. Thought needs now to be given by progressive Catholics and Protestants, as to how the Evangelical Insurrection can become increasingly ecumenical. Thought needs also to be given, by Christians in western countries, as to how the Evangelical Insurrection can be helped to happen here. It is one of the means by which Incarnation is happening in Nicaragua.

As I have said, behind the ecclesiastical, political and theological debates in Nicaragua is a profound disagreement as to the meaning of the Incarnation. It is the difference between a belief in a God-out-there and a God-in-here, belief in a Christ who looks on helplessly at poverty and injustice and a Christ who engages in the struggle to change them, belief in a salvation which humanity is powerless to initiate and one which God and human beings together battle to create. There is a theology of death and a theology of the dawn. Western Christians need to know, for our own theological struggles, what is happening, both in thought and practice, in Nicaragua.

# 6

# Learning from Nicaragua – A Faith for Today

The prevailing view of western Christians is still that we have much to teach or to contribute to the developing countries, the 'Third World', the nations of Asia, Africa and Latin America. In fact an increasing number now believe the reverse to be true – that we have much more to learn from those countries than to teach them, and that we desperately need to hear their missionary message. One of the reasons why we are not hearing this message is that they do not have the resources to communicate it to us. We either have to bring Christians here from such countries, or go there to learn. Many Christians in the West feel very strongly that there are essential contributions to be made by Christians from Asia, Africa and Latin America to the salvation of the church and indeed of the world, without which we shall be quite unable to progress in the primary tasks in which God seeks to participate with us. Later in this chapter I shall outline the kind of lessons we can learn in the Nicaraguan context in the areas of theology, spirituality, prophecy and discipleship. Perhaps first however should come a comment on the relevance of the struggle between the different motivations and ideologies. It is important at this point to make it clear that when I refer to 'Nicaraguan Christians' I have in mind those progressive Christians who are committed to the struggle for the new society in Nicaragua.

### *The Ideological Struggle*

The battle that is going on more generally between quite different perceptions of the nature of Christianity, the purpose of the church and the meaning of the gospel, is perhaps at its sharpest in Nicaragua today. Many western Christians suggest that these differences are not all that great and that Christians with different approaches agree much more than they disagree. In the more polarized environment of Nicaragua, where such differences can and have made the difference between life and death, that suggestion can be seen to be superficial. That is not to say that different interpretations of Christianity have nothing in common, and that those espousing them are irrevocably irreconcilable, but it does mean the differences are profound and cannot easily be brushed aside. Christians of both the conservative evangelical, or even fundamentalist, persuasion and those espousing a radical or liberationist theology need to recognize this, as do those who claim to be somewhere in the middle.

Those conservative Christians who stress the importance of converting individuals to Christianity in order to improve the world have been seeking to accomplish that in the western capitalist context now for at least two hundred years. They appear to have been singularly unsuccessful. Nicaragua is an example of how the depredations of the Spanish, English and North Americans have brought mainly exploitation, conflict and death, culminating in the particularly vicious Somoza dictatorship of the 1960s and 1970s. The Sandinistas, in a matter of six years, have provided more education, health care, housing and land for the *campesinos* than the forty-five years of the Somocistas, despite the latters' claim to Christianity and their backing from the most powerful Christian nation in history. As one Nicaraguan pastor commented, 'I support the revolution because I see it doing in just a short time what the church has been *saying* it wanted to do for hundreds of years.'[1]

The message from Nicaragua is that the structures have to be changed before the work of bringing justice can truly begin. Does not that experience have very profound implications for the beliefs and practices of Christians in capitalist societies? It is time for Christians to realize that western Christendom may have led to that most terrifying state of sinfulness, the denial – even the negation – of a true and whole gospel.

### *Contextual Theology*

The theology emerging in Nicaragua – as of course in many other situations of struggle – makes clear the absolute necessity of evolving a theology which as well as being rooted in the Bible and the history and doctrine of the church is also firmly related to the context in which Christians are living. It is crucial to study the history, the social, political and economic structures, the role the church has actually played and the values and hopes of a society before what God seeks in that situation can be understood, before an adequate and effective theology can be developed and the gospel role of the church fully discerned. Nicaraguan Protestants through CEPRES, CEPAD and the CAV are busily working out such a theology, to be expressed in both belief and practice.

In the case of Nicaragua, as I hope I have demonstrated in this book, it is necessary to comprehend historically such questions as the differences between the Pacific and Atlantic coastal regions, the conflicts between the interests of different racial groups, the effects of North American involvement and the relative positions of the Catholic and Protestant churches. Without this information how can God helpfully be heard and his mission properly understood? If for example the theme of reconciliation is being studied theologically, how can this be done in Nicaragua without referring to the differences between the various racial groups, and how these might best be overcome? The same would apply to such a study in the UK, the USA or many European countries. When the Nicaraguans study the meaning of the Cross, they draw clear links between the events of the crucifixion and their own experience. That may be more difficult for western Christians, but there are clear parallels in the experiences of the dispossessed in our societies; their oppression and suffering increases as soon as they begin to seek their rights. The parallels are there if we have eyes to see and ears to hear.

Turning to the structures of society, Nicaraguan Christians in the 1960s and 1970s, along with non-Christians inside and outside the Sandinista movement, were beginning to investigate what was actually going on in their nation. Who owned the businesses, the land, the other forms of capital? What effect was this having on the rest of the people? The conclusion they came to was quite clear, that the majority of the nation's resources were owned by a tiny, élite group of its members and that this was totally unacceptable, on either Christian or humanitarian grounds. The fact that Marxists came to the same conclusion from the same information is not without significance. Hence this situation had to be changed, peacefully if possible but perhaps not, if the privileged used violence to avoid sharing their wealth with the poor. An effective Nicaraguan theology has to engage with this kind of thinking, and this kind of experience. And again this is all sufficiently close to the western situation for us to have a good deal upon which to meditate.

What does the Bible say about it? Are there any similar situations in the history of the church? What does God say about the structures of injustice and the nature of the struggle to change them? The picture of God that emerges from biblical and historical study is of a God determined to have such structures demolished, a God willing to participate with his people in the efforts to win the changes, willing to join the suffering of the ensuing struggle, and even painfully and regretfully willing ultimately to countenance armed confrontation if the rich and powerful resist. Those who say there is no biblical precedent can be pointed to the bloody exodus of Israel from Egypt with the deaths of the first-born and the drowning of Pharoah's army, the even bloodier annexing of the Promised Land of Canaan, the military conquests of King David of whose line Jesus came and the fearless confronting by Jesus of the principalities and powers of Rome and the Temple, even if he himself saw his role as on another plane from leading an armed revolt. We are not Jesus, say Nicaraguan Christians, we had to work out what to do as Christians when our people were being crucified daily. Some of us took up arms although some could not. But many, many of us supported the revolutionary struggle. Miguel d'Escoto has expressed the ambivalence felt by many Christians over this issue, but his conclusion is clear. And if we in the West do not want Nicaragua to resort to violence to defend itself, we have to work out ways of stopping the attacks upon it.

Our white, western, academic theology can avoid such choices because our context is not apparently one of struggle. Our dominant theology portrays a god who agonizes over a world where societies spend far more on weapons than on bread for the poor, in which a possessive materialism becomes the driving force, in which the rich get richer and the poor struggle to survive. Should that not be a context of struggle, if it is not already?

## *Practical Spirituality*

Spirituality is a term much more discussed among contemporary Christians than a few decades ago. It refers to the form in which personal faith is practised, to the way the Spirit is experienced in the thoughts and activities of the believer. Until recently it was relegated to a lower place by radical Christians because of its connotations of piety, individualism, much Bible study and private prayer, without any real relationship with practical action. Nicaraguan Christians, like some in other areas of struggle, for example southern Africa, seem to have experienced a breakthrough in bringing together these two areas of the Christian life, the spiritual and the practical. For them their Bible study is closely related to their experience and activity, their prayer is a building of spiritual strength for the continuing struggle, their worship is an expressing of God's incarnation in this struggle and not simply in the world of two thousand years ago. There is still of course much traditional worship and prayer in Nicaragua, but among progressive Baptists and Catholics, for example, there is a spirituality much more related to life's demands.

Bible study is particularly important. It appears to be much more alive in the Nicaraguan context for those involved in it. There is a rediscovery of the Bible as a book which speaks of injustice, struggle, economic analysis, fundamental change and genuine hope. 'It seems to be because here people really live the Bible stories,' said one foreign church worker, speaking about how Nicaragua used to be and how El Salvador is still:

> For example in the Christmas story, when this poor young *campesina* (peasant woman) had to go off scores of miles to register

> because the authorities said so, the people in Central America know exactly what that means; when she has to give birth to her baby in a cattle-shed, they've experienced that too; when the soldiers come to murder the child, they all know someone who's been in that kind of situation; when a little family has to flee into a foreign country to escape persecution, that rings many bells as well. Here, the Bible is alive.[2]

So the Bible becomes a much more personal, meaningful source of experience and guidance than in wealthy western societies. Perhaps the best way for us to understand this process at a distance is to study *The Gospel in Solentiname*, the books by Ernesto Cardenal to which I referred to in chapter three. The spirituality of Central American Christians has become something which incorporates experience, reflection and active participation in the struggle. It is a spirituality in which a God of struggle, suffering and hope becomes meaningful and real instead of a divinity understood as our personal protector and redeemer and our cosy undemanding soul-mate. It is a spirituality which both challenges and enables Christians to analyse and oppose structures of injustice and domination no matter what the consequences, which discerns the movement of the spirit in movements for social and economic change, and locates Christian discipleship there. Indeed it is a spirituality which cannot rest while unjust structures remain, for it sees them as deeply destructive of human dignity and therefore atheistic, a real and manifest rejection of God.

### *Prophecy – Naming the Beast*

The Christians of Nicaragua are in a much better position than we are to see who and what is holding up the development of God's kingdom in which all may be one. They are very clear about the Christian nature of the project of the revolution, and the forces which are seeking to halt or overthrow it. They are often much more willing than we are, particularly in personal conversation, to be unequivocal about who is attempting to destroy them and why. They are more specific than the Christian community whose thinking is enshrined in the Revelation of St. John, who spoke of the Beast, and described him in code, but did not actually name him. It is in fact the role of the prophets throughout the Bible (of whom the apocalyptic Johannine community could be said to be the last) to draw attention to the powers which are acting in opposition to God's will and preventing the coming of the kingdom. In this context the Christians of Nicaragua have the important role of identifying and naming such powers in today's world.

The simplest phrase to describe what the Nicaraguan Christians see as the Beast is 'US imperialism', that is the arrogant, greedy, dominating use of power, and the search for even greater power, by the administration of the United States, backed by the military, industrial and financial interests which are at the heart of the modern US empire. That empire is determined to retain and if possible expand its power, its wealth and its status in the world at all costs. The behaviour of a small Latin American country having the insolence first to overthrow the leadership that the US had designated for it and then reject the new instructions subsequently given is not to be tolerated.

There are, too, interest-groups in the United States which, as well as objecting to a small nation's insolence, fear that the example of Nicaragua might put similar ideas into the heads of the people in other larger and economically more important countries. Then US interests might be more seriously threatened than by a free Nicaragua. The United States depends considerably on both the raw materials and the financial returns it reaps from the countries of Latin America. If they all begin to develop political and economic independence, from where will the cheap agricultural and mineral products come, upon which the US relies? Who will provide the huge debt repayments that North America is regularly extracting from the countries of the South? Which military régimes will buy the enormous variety of US hardware on sale to keep the continent divided and ruled?

In the light of such fears, extreme action seems justifiable in the defence of US interests to those who benefit from US imperialism. Economic sabotage and boycott, propaganda and downright lies, subverting the disaffected losers from the new just order, equipping and training of a terrorist mercenary army – many members of which were the vicious and oppressive arm of the previous brutal dictatorship, are among the tactics being used in Nicaragua. To many the fear of Communism seems a wholly inadequate excuse, even if the Soviet Union were half as bad as the US government paints it. The present United States leadership has plumbed the depths of both ignorance and immorality in its desperate efforts to justify its bullying, brutal, terrorist attacks on the tiny nation of Nicaragua. Those Christians there who correctly identify the nature of the Beast are strongly committed to the struggle against it. Some speak and write, some help the people to organize themselves, some educate the Christian community, some train and fight and die. It is true that some North Americans and Europeans have also named the Beast and joined the struggle, but are they not still far too few, and far too timid?

### *Discipleship*

The qualities required of followers of Jesus are strength and warmth of character, sensitivity, unyielding courage, humanity and suffering love. The Christians of Nicaragua display all of these, in differing quantities at differing times. The strength and courage is needed in response to the economic and military pressures on the country, where things could be so much more constructive if the economy were allowed to evolve as planned (with the same loan and credit facilities as other nearby countries enjoy); the 40% – 50% of the budget required for defence delays and destroys so many scheduled improvements for the nation's poor. The sensitivity is shown when, despite the Nicaraguans' clear understanding about what is being done to them, they offer a continued welcome for North American and other western Christians to their country, and they locate blame for their predicament with the US government rather than its people. They exhibit great humanity despite their considerable achievements and seek no plaudits for offering the world a way forward out of poverty, injustice and despair. Suffering love enables them often to regard their aggressors with amused despair, though it is clear there is also a (divine) sense of wrath engendered by the enormous damage being done to their country.

It is a humbling exercise to read again Bonhoeffer's *Cost of Discipleship* in the context of what faces not just the Christians of Nicaragua but the whole nation. It was Bonhoeffer who inspired the first young Baptists to identify with the revolutionary cause, because he recognized, perhaps more than any other white western male theologian, the nature of the faith in the secular age, the depth of discipleship that Jesus requires and the potential for evil in western societies.

There are however some ways in which western Christians have responded to the example of the discipleship being offered by the Christians of Nicaragua. Two of these are the Witness for Peace programme and the Pledge of Resistance. Under the auspices of Witness for Peace groups of Christians (mostly North American) travel to Nicaragua for anything from a week to a year, and spend a period of time alongside the Nicaraguans in the war zones, running the risks of the *contra* raids and attacks. They aim to form what they call a 'shield of care'. They gather information on *contra* activity and publish descriptions of atrocities committed, such as *What We Have Seen and Heard.*[3] They are aged from twenty to seventy and by August 1986 over 2000 had participated in the programme. The Pledge of Resistance is a statement signed by those in western countries who are willing, if the United States appears to be invading Nicaragua, to undertake actions of non-violent civil disobedience which will cause enormous disruption in US government affairs throughout the world, and severely embarrass any US administration which attempts to take such a step. By 1986 the Pledge had 80,000 signatories in the USA, and having begun in late 1985 in the UK as a rather less demanding Pledge of Witness had achieved a total of 1,000 signatures, the majority of these being in Scotland.

## *Faith in Struggle*

I have been seeking to show that there are many crucial lessons which Christians in other parts of the world have to learn from the progressive Christians of Nicaragua. If we seek to learn them effectively they may well bring disagreement, misunderstanding and polarization as they have done within the Nicaraguan churches. In this context we may come to a new understanding of sayings of Jesus such as 'I have not come to bring peace but a sword.' But it is essential for western Christians to embrace the theology of the dawn. Much of our Christianity has become moribund and superficial. We are too busy asking Christians in Nicaragua and elsewhere how they practise their faith effectively in a socialist society without coming to terms with the practical impossibility of doing so in a capitalist one. How, when Christians can plainly see the exploitation, injustice and oppression caused by the West's economic systems, both in our own countries and elsewhere, can we restrain ourselves from seeking to challenge it and to institute processes of fundamental change?

One of the most crucial lessons from Nicaragua is therefore the example of partnership between progressive Christians and the socialists and Marxists of the Sandinista movement. It offers a paradigm for exploring the practical implications of living out the faith in society. The Sandinistas offer a social and economic programme, the Christians some insights on how best to carry it out. They should be able to, after all, if they are being sensitive and faithful to the prompting of the Spirit. But the Nicaraguan Christians are only able to engage in this way because they first participated in the liberation struggle. And they participated partly because they read their Bible contextually, but also because the Sandinistas asked them to. A Christian presence was wanted in the struggle, and it gave the Christians the chance to test the reality of their faith. And most of them did not draw back when the barricades went up and the bullets began to fly. Not all of them felt able to take up arms. Nevertheless, their commitment won them the right to participate in the formation of the new society. They took up the Cross and so were offered the opportunity to share in the experience of resurrection. The struggle continues today in Nicaragua over the nature of the faith.

It is perhaps in the concept of struggle that we discover the most important lesson of all from the Nicaraguans. In this concept are contained the themes of commitment, opposition to evil, suffering and hope. It is a concept which an increasing number of Christians in a wide range of countries engaged in practising the faith are using.

It surfaces in southern Africa, North America, Asia and Europe. For example Ed de la Torre from the Philippines in his book published in July 1986 *Touching Ground, Taking Root* writes of 'companions in the struggle' and makes much use of the concept in his essays on the emerging theology of progressive Filipino Christians.[4] It is clear that in the struggle against the forces of selfishness, reaction and oppression the Christian faith becomes more fully understood. We western Christians therefore need urgently to commit ourselves more fully to the struggle, against imperialism, militarization and oppression and for liberation, justice and peace. We need more faith in the struggle, for it is in the struggle that we discover the faith.

# *Appendix 1*

## Statement from the Moravian Church of Nicaragua

| | |
|---|---|
| *From:* | The Seventh Triennial Synod of the Moravian Church of Nicaragua. |
| *To:* | The Government of Nicaragua and the Groups under Arms, the Moravian Community in Nicaragua, all Nicaraguans, and the Ecumenical Community, national and international. |
| *Reference:* | Dialogue, Reconciliation, Justice and Peace |
| *Date:* | 20 February 1986, Puerto Cabezas, Nicaragua |

All we delegates of the various towns of the Moravian community in Nicaragua, at the Seventh Triennial Synod, in session from 11 February to 20 February 1986 in the town of Puerto Cabezas, Zelaya Norte, declare our profound concern over the situation of our peoples of the Atlantic Coast and of all Nicaragua. The last five years have been a very difficult period.

We have experienced grief, suffering, displacements, destruction, family break-up, and death, and have been unable to enjoy the most elemental rights of life, because of an unjust war, unnecessarily imposed by forces foreign to our Nicaraguan reality. Today more than before we are conscious that the war serves only to break down and not to build up.

We have listened to the complete outcry from our people, from workers, professionals, youth, children and from the parties in violent conflict: 'we want peace', 'we are tired of war'. Therefore we invite the government of Nicaragua, and the Nicaraguans in armed conflict against the government, to seek a fraternal dialogue, responsible and sincere, with the aim of reaching a dignified reconciliation, social justice and a lasting peace.

At the same time we demand that forces external and foreign to our situation cease immediately their support for violence and instead employ their influence to promote peace.

As a church, we assure our people, our government and all Nicaraguans in this armed conflict we are with them in whatever efforts are necessary for obtaining peace, as this is still the central message of the holy gospel, 'Glory to God in the highest, and peace on earth to people of goodwill' (Luke 2.14).

In the same way we guarantee our total support for the process of autonomy for the Atlantic coast of Nicaragua as the coastal people have demanded, making a call to our people and to all the Nicaraguan citizens of the Atlantic coast to participate actively in the discussion towards reaching a genuine autonomy within the spirit of unity in the Nicaraguan nation. We invite all our congregations, the people of Nicaragua, the ecumenical community national and international, to accompany us in maintaining wisdom, intercessory prayer and the pastoral work of consolation, 'Console one another,' says Paul.

God bless you and keep you, God lift up his face upon you and grant you mercy, God raise his countenance upon you and give you peace.

Amen

(Author's Translation)

# *Appendix 2*

## Pastoral Letter from the Board of Directors of the Baptist Convention of Nicaragua

4 July 1986

THE AMERICAN BAPTIST CHURCHES OF THE UNITED STATES

THE SOUTHERN BAPTIST CONVENTION OF THE UNITED STATES

THE WORLD BAPTIST ALLIANCE

CHRISTIANS OF THE UNITED STATES

Beloved brothers and sisters in Christ:

We address you in the midst of the very grave situation created by the approval of the $110 million by the United States Congress for the Nicaraguan counter-revolution. This measure entails a financing of pain, of death, and of the destruction of our suffering people. Nevertheless, for us this approval is something more than a violation of International Law by the Reagan administration: it is the advancement of the dominion of darkness over light, the imposition of death over life, and force over reason and justice. In spite of this advancement, we are encouraged by the biblical promise that darkness cannot prevail over light (John 1.5).

Because of the economic embargo against Nicaragua, the war imposed by the White House through the counter-revolution and the disinformation campaigns and pressures against this country, life is becoming almost impossible here: the food supply is alarmingly scarce, the most elemental medicines are lacking, transportation is precarious, raw materials, spare parts, job possibilities are more difficult each day. Daily we bury and weep over our dead while diseases, malnutrition and desperation spread among our people.

As Christians we ask ourselves: what right does the most powerful and rich nation of the world have to impose misery, pain and death on a poor and weak people like Nicaragua? What right does the Reagan administration have to decide the destiny of Nicaragua?

Beloved brothers and sisters in Christ: the gospel that you taught us through the missionaries speaks to us of the construction of life, of love, of comprehension. In base of this model we have pledged ourselves to reconstruct our nation, destroyed by earthquakes and wars. Now, this same gospel that you brought us, that speaks to us of a just God – loathes injustice and loves and brings forth life, obliges us to address and ask you once again to raise the banner of justice and to defend the life and right of 'the least of these' (Matthew 25.40), the Nicaraguans.

Beloved brothers and sisters: if the United States were to live the situation that Nicaragua actually lives, you would be experiencing the death of 1,467,000 people; you would have 733,500 orphans, 16,000,000 refugees, billions of dollars in lost materials and dozens more horrifying figures. How would you feel if a country a hundred times more powerful than you were to declare war against you? Be it far from us to desire for you such a great tragedy. Nevertheless, beloved brothers and sisters, this is a sad reality for us: as three million Nicaraguans we suffer the unspeakable as a result of the policies of the Reagan administration towards this country. Only one example: yesterday, on 3 July, thirty-two people perished, of which twelve were children and twelve were women, victims of an anti-tank mine cruelly manipulated by remote control. This is what your government is fomenting against us Nicaraguans.

The apostle Paul invites us to make our sufferings known to our brothers and sisters (Romans 12.15), but more than that, the Word calls us to defend those who suffer because of the powerful: 'THE KIND OF FASTING I WANT IS THIS: REMOVE THE CHAINS OF OPPRESSION AND THE YOKE OF INJUSTICE, AND LET THE OPPRESSED GO FREE' (Isaiah 58.6 GNB).

We consider that God has spoken and that he has manifested

himself in a very clear manner with the decision of the World Court of Justice of the Hague, this past 27 June. This Court is the highest international tribunal, co-founded by the United States. In fact, the United States has turned to this tribunal thirteen times in order to settle diverse problems. The World Court condemned the United States as a violator of International Law in its policy against Nicaragua and ordered it to detain the aggression and the war and to compensate Nicaragua for the serious damage to our economy. Unfortunately, it will never be possible to compensate our people for the 20,000 deaths and the profound pain of our mothers.

Nevertheless, the Reagan administration has disregarded and ignored the decision of the World Court and has set out to continue financing war and death. How many schools, health centres, highways could be constructed in Nicaragua with this money? How many children could we vaccinate and save from the terrible diseases that we inherited from the Somoza dictatorship? So much 'abundant life' could be made possible for our people with these funds! Sadly so, this money is destined to continue the hurting and the destroying the hopes of life that still remain in Nicaragua. The next step could well be the direct intervention of United States forces, that would convert Nicaragua into a vast cemetery, full of Nicaraguan and United States people.

This aggressive policy of the United States obliges us to live in a permanent state of emergency in order to defend ourselves from those who are sending death and destruction. Although this measure is not an obstacle for the work of our pastors and churches, nor for the Nicaraguans who love this country, it does cause difficulties in the development of a normal life. Our prayer to the Lord is that the aggression ceases so that we can live with tranquillity and reconstruct our nation.

Our preoccupation, nevertheless, beloved brothers and sisters, does not end just with the pain, death and desperation of our suffering people. Rather we suffer and we are worried for you because we consider that the Reagan administration is undermining life, not only in Nicaragua, but also in your own nation. Those noble principles brandished by you on the glorious 4 July 1776, 210 years ago, principles that appeal to life, to justice, to dignity, to sovereignty, to liberty, are being trampled: of evil, good is spoken (the destroyers of life are called 'freedom fighters', to overthrow a legitimate government is to laud democracy); and of the good, evil is spoken (the reconstruction of our country, the praising of human values, literacy, health, equality is described as a 'Communist dictatorship'). Judicial law that governs all civilized society is put to one side and in its stead 'might makes right' governs as it did 8000 years ago. Instead of encouraging peace, war is fomented; in the place of life, death.

When neither law or righteousness or reason or Christian conscience can overcome, all that remains is the just judgment of God which is justice. To God all will have to respond for the unpunished shedding of innocent blood: 'THEN THE LORD SAID, "WHY HAVE YOU DONE THIS TERRIBLE THING? YOUR BROTHER'S BLOOD IS CRYING OUT TO ME FROM THE GROUND, LIKE A VOICE CALLING FOR JUSTICE" ' (Genesis 4.10 GNB).

Beloved brothers and sisters: now is the time of reflexion and of turning back to those Christian values that the gospel demands of us; now is the hour to do justice with the people of Nicaragua, before it is too late for you and for us, before (and without any exaggeration) all life is extinguished in Nicaragua.

We are grateful to our brothers and sisters of the United States who have demonstrated with words and acts their support and solidarity with the cause of the Nicaraguan people. At the same time we encourage them to continue forward with the struggle of life, justice and peace.

Conscious of the errors that we as Nicaraguans have committed, and of our role to correct those errors, we ask you as brothers and sisters in Christ and members of his great family, ACT SO THAT THE UNITED STATES GOVERNMENT WILL LEAVE US IN PEACE AND WILL RETURN TO US THE RIGHT TO LIVE IN PEACE. ACT SO THAT THE DECISION OF THE WORLD COURT OF THE HAGUE WILL BE HEARD AND OBEYED.

With that faith and confidence that the Lord will move soon through you and through other means, in our favour, we write you with the hope that comes from the highest God: 'FOR YOU THE LORD

IS A SAFE RETREAT; YOU HAVE MADE THE MOST HIGH YOUR REFUGE' (Psalms 91.9 NEB).

Fraternally,
THE BOARD OF DIRECTORS
OF THE BAPTIST CONVENTION OF NICARAGUA

| | | |
|---|---|---|
| Rev. Eugenio Zamora<br>President | Marilyn Méndez<br>Secretary | Tomás Téllez R.<br>Executive Secretary |
| Gonzalo Mairena<br>Vocal | Flor de Zavala<br>President Bp. Women | Cony de Méndez<br>Promotor Education |
| Pablo García<br>Promot. Finances | Félix Ruiz<br>Presid. Evangelism | Sergio Denis García<br>Presid. Planifica. |
| Candelaria de Zamora<br>Presid. Home for Aged | Jerjes Ruiz<br>Ministerial Alliance | Roberto López D.<br>Baptist School |
| Roberto Córdoba<br>Vocal | Róger González B.<br>Centro Bautista | Javier Talavera<br>Promotor of Youth |
| Róger Zavala B.<br>Rector Seminary | Manuel Zamora<br>Treasurer | Elías Sánchez<br>Vice-President |
| Gustavo Parajón<br>Presid. Baptist Miss. | Francisco Juarez<br>Presid. Chrst. Serv. | Lidia García<br>Promotor Bapt. Women |

cc: World Council of Churches
Christian bodies around the world

# *Appendix 3*

## Diocesan Statement by the Episcopal (Anglican) Church of Nicaragua, Bluefields, September 1984

The 14th Diocesan Convention of the Episcopal Church of Nicaragua (Anglican) convened in Bluefields during the days of 19 November and 20 November, 1983, hereby made known to the people of Nicaragua, the following:

considering that our government and people have demonstrated their desire for peace and goodwill internationally, and

considering that the United Nations, the Organization of the American States, and the Group of Contadora comprised of Mexico, Venezuela, Colombia and Panama have recommended political and not military solutions in the region, and,

considering that the above organizations have recommended non-intervention of the world's power groups in the Central American area and the removal of foreign military forces in the Central American countries, and

considering that Nicaragua is constantly being assaulted, with strong possibilities of an invasion, and

considering that the attacks from both north and south of our frontiers have caused large losses in our economy and in human lives, and

considering that the Reagan administration has publicly admitted US aid to the contra revolutionaries with money and arms and the US intention to destroy the Nicaragua revolution, and

considering that the economic assistance given by the Reagan administration is in open violation of actual international laws, and

considering that the Nicaraguan government has made concrete proposals of peace to the Reagan administration as well as to the governments and people of Central America,

we hereby resolve on the following:

to condemn most energetically the economic and military aggression of the Reagan administration toward Nicaragua, and also other countries that are contributing to this political interference in the matters of other states;

to make an appeal to the entire Anglican Communion and especially to other churches in Central America, that they do all they possibly can to influence their members, their communities and their governments to help in the steps taken for peace in Central America and by so doing avoid war among brothers; and

that each member of the Episcopal Church of Nicaragua try to defend by concrete actions the lives and future of our children, our youth, and our aged people, showing love toward our fellowmen, as our church teaches us to do.

May the peace of God be with all the people of Central America.

# *Appendix 4*

## Pastoral Letter from the General Assembly of CEPAD to the Peoples and Churches of the World

(Approved unanimously by the General Assembly of CEPAD, 17 July, 1986.)

Beloved of God who are called to be saints, may God our Father and the Lord Jesus Christ send you grace and peace (Romans 1.7).

We write this letter to you because the decision in the Congress of the United States on 25 June to approve funds for the counter-revolution will only escalate the belligerent aggression against Nicaragua. This decision will increase the suffering and cause the death of many of our people.

We address ourselves especially to our sisters and brothers in Christ. We believe that Christ is the bond that unites us, breaking down whatever geographic frontiers, ideological exclusivism or political intolerance divide us (Ephesians 2.4). Both you who profess Christ in other countries as well as we, Nicaraguan Christians, have a vocation above whatever terrestial citizenship we possess. We are primarily citizens of the Reign of God (Philippians 3.20), and thus affirm with John Wesley that 'the world is our parish'.

As a part, therefore, of the universal church, the pilgrim people of the Lord, we are called to obedience to God and to the cultivation of brotherhood and sisterhood in our respective societies, working always for the fullness of life.

Thus we are called to raise our voice from Nicaragua, a small country siezed by anguish and uncertainty. The decision by the Nicaraguan people to forge our own destiny has provoked a hostile reaction from the government of the United States of America.

Responding to our historic action with an escalating war and an economic embargo, the US aggression has born fruit in over 17,000 dead, 12,000 orphans, hundreds of widows, 250,000 people displaced from their homes by the war; the destruction of bridges, health centres, schools, production centres and electrical facilities; the mining of roads and ports; and a severe shortage of food, basic medicines, clothing, shoes, etc.

We have recently observed, with amazement, the US refusal to recognize the competency of the International Court of Justice in The Hague. The Court ruled in Nicaragua's favour, condemning the illegitimate policy of the United States and ordering the US to indemnify Nicaragua for damages caused by the war. We lament this evasion of justice by the US.

Inasmuch as we believe it is our human and pastoral responsibility to defend the orphan, the exploited, and the widow – who are protected by Yahweh (Deuteronomy 10.18; Psalms 10.18, 68.5);

And, inasmuch as we, as Christians, citizens of the Reign of God, are called to give good news to the poor (Luke 4.18,19) and to proclaim the message of justice, peace, and love that comes from the cross of Christ (II Corinthians 5.18–20);

And, inasmuch as the people of Nicaragua are poor and suffer in their own flesh the cruel effects of a war of aggression conceived and directed from outside our country;

Therefore:

1. We call upon our sisters and brothers in Christ around the world to use your spiritual resources so that the war against us – directed by those who make the foreign policy of the United States – will stop, and that the leaders of Nicaragua will continue to faithfully govern, uplifting the collective good of our nation (II Corinthians 5.20).

2. We proclaim before the world our commitment to maintain dialogue with local churches, international church bodies and assistance agencies in order to search for and nurture the fellowship of the Spirit, in order that we make a common response that

will assist the Nicaraguan people in their struggle for wholeness (I Timothy 2.1,2).

3. We urge our sisters and brothers in other countries to overcome all narrow nationalism and ideology in order to unanimously respond, in the liberating and loving spirit of the gospel, to a people being slaughtered by foreign aggression (I Peter 2.9).

4. We propose a campaign of prayer, fasting, and whatever similar activities are possible, designed to intercede before God so that the war imposed on Nicaragua will stop and peace will be achieved (Psalms 34:4, Jeremiah 29.11).

Finally, we express our gratitude to those of you who, in one form or another, continue giving us moral, spiritual, and material aid in this time of Nicaragua's suffering. Today, more than ever, we need your firm support.

'Glory be to him whose power, working in us, can do infinitely more than we can ask or imagine; glory be to him from generation to generation in the church and in Christ Jesus for ever and ever. Amen' (Ephesians 3.20–21).

Shalom!

Signed for the General Assembly by the Executive Board:
Dr Gustavo A. Parajón, President;
Rev. Enrique Palacios, Vice-President;
Rev. Alejandro Duarte, Treasurer;
and Thelma de Pereira and Rev. Anastasio Martinez, members.

# *Appendix 5*

## Christians in Nicaragua's Sandinist Revolution*

For some time the enemies of our people after being driven from power have been carrying on a pernicious campaign of misinterpretation and lies about various aspects of the revolution with the intention of creating confusion. This ideological confusion is an attempt to arouse fear and anti-Sandinist attitudes and wear down the FSLN's political base in endless polemics without concern for justice.

In these campaigns to sow confusion, the subject of religion occupies a prominent place. This is to be expected, since a high percentage of Nicaraguans are deeply religious. The forces of reaction try to sell the idea that the FSLN is making use of religion at this time with the idea of suppressing it later on. It is clear that the purpose of the campaigns is to manipulate the people's humble faith in order to provoke a political reaction against the FSLN and the revolution.

The campaigns are especially perverse because they deal with matters that strike deep sentiments of many Nicaraguans. Given the importance of the subject, and in order to orient our members, clarify things for our people and prevent further manipulation of this matter, the National Directorate of the FSLN has decided to set forth in this document its official position on religion.

Patriotic revolutionary Christians are members of the Sandinist Popular Revolution and have been for many years. The participation

*Translated by James and Margaret Goff (CAV). This is not a government or official translation.

of Christians, both lay-people and religious, in the FSLN and in the National Reconstruction Government (GRN) is a logical consequence of their outstanding identification with the people throughout the struggle against the dictatorship.

### *Faith Motivates Participation*

Many FSLN members and combatants found in the interpretation of the faith their motivation to become part of the revolutionary struggle and consequently of the FSLN. Many of them gave very courageous help to our cause and were exemplary in their willingness to die and shed their blood to make the seed of liberation grow. How can we forget our beloved martyrs, such as Oscar Pérez Cassar, Oscar Robelo, Sergio Guerrero, Arlen Siu, Guadalupe Moreno and Leonardo Matute, and the dozens of Delegates of the Word assassinated in the mountains by members of Somoza's National Guard, besides many more of our brothers and sisters.

Special mention must be made of the heroic sacrifice of Gaspar García Laviana, a Catholic priest and Sandinist member, in whom Christian vocation and revolutionary awareness were synthesized to the highest degree. They were all humble people who knew how to perform their duty as patriots and revolutionaries without getting involved in long philosophical discussions. Today they live eternally in the memory of the people, who will never forget their sacrifice.

But the participation of Christians was not limited to their contribution as combatants in the Sandinist Front. Many Christians – lay and religious – who never joined the FSLN ranks, although some of them were related to it, preached and practised their faith in conjunction with the needs for liberating our people. Even the institutional Catholic church and some Protestant churches participated in the popular victory over Somoza's reign of terror.

### *Christian Collaboration*

On several occasions the Catholic bishops valiantly denounced the dictatorship's crimes and abuses, especially Bishops (Miguel) Obando y Bravo and (Manuel) Salazar y Espinoza who, among others, suffered the harassment of Somoza's forces for doing so. It was a group of priests and sisters who denounced to the world the disappearance of 3,000 *campesinos* in the northern mountainous region. Many Christians of different denominations carried a liberating message to the people. There were also those who gave refuge and food to the Sandinists who were being persecuted and killed by Somoza's forces. It was in the churches that the people met to hear news from the underground when Somoza's repression kept independent radio stations from broadcasting.

For this valiant participation in the struggle the Catholic church and Christians in general met persecution and death. In the same way, many religious suffered harassment. Some were expelled; others were kept from practising their Christian faith in a thousand different ways; many churches were profaned, sacked, bombed and attacked to kill *compañeros* within, as occurred, for example, in El Calvario Church in León and in chapels in the mountains.

Thus Christians have been an integral part of our revolutionary history to a degree without precedence in any other revolutionary movement of Latin America and possibly of the world. This fact opens new and interesting possibilities for Christian participation in revolutions of other lands, not only in the period of the struggle for power but also in the next stage, that of the construction of a new society.

We revolutionary Christians and non-Christians must dedicate ourselves to the task of giving continuity and projection into the future of this very valuable experience under the new conditions which the revolutionary process sets out for us. We must perfect ways leading to aware participation among all revolutionaries of Nicaragua, irrespective of their philosophical position and religious belief.

## *FSLN Policy on Religion*

*Freedom to profess religious faith* 1. For the FSLN, freedom to profess a religious faith is an inalienable human right which the Revolutionary Government fully guarantees. This principle has been written into our Revolutionary Program for a long time and we will uphold it effectively in the future. But what is more, no one is to be discriminated against in the new Nicaragua for publicly professing or propagating his or her religious beliefs. Those who do not profess a religious faith also have this right.

*Revolutionary activity can spring from faith* 2. Some writers have said that religion is a tool for the alienation of people and serves to justify the exploitation of one class by another. This affirmation no doubt has historical value to the degree that in other historical periods religion offered theoretical support for political domination. It is enough to recall the role of missionaries in the process of the domination and colonization of the Indians of our country.

However, as Sandinists we affirm that our experience has shown that when Christians, standing on their faith, are capable of responding to the needs of people and history, their beliefs drive them to revolutionary activity. Our experience shows that it is possible to be a believer and a committed revolutionary at the same time and that there is no irreconcilable contradiction between the two.

*Party membership open to revolutionary Christians* 3. The FSLN is an organization of Nicaraguan revolutionaries who have united voluntarily to transform the social, economic and political reality of our country by following a programme and a recognized strategy. All who agree with our objectives and purposes and have the personal qualities that our organization requires have every right to join our ranks, irrespective of their religious beliefs. Proof of this is the participation in the Sandinist Assembly of three Catholic priests. Many Christians belong to the FSLN, and as long as there are revolutionary Christians in Nicaragua there will be Christians in the Sandinist Front.

*Inside FSLN partisan structure, no room for proselytism; outside, yes* 4. The FSLN as the vanguard, aware of the immense responsibility that has fallen on its shoulders, jealously watches over the unity and strength of its organization around the objectives for which it has expressly been constituted. In the FSLN's partisan structure there is no room for religious proselytism, inasmuch as that would pervert the special character of our vanguard and introduce divisive forces; already, *compañeros* of differing or no religious belief are brought together in the Sandinista Front. Outside the partisan framework Christians, whether priests, pastors, men or women religious, or lay-people, have every right publicly to express their convictions without limiting their membership of the FSLN or diminishing the confidence they have gained from their revolutionary work.

*Religious traditions respected* 5. The FSLN has profound respect for all the religious celebrations and traditions of our people and endeavours to rescue the true meaning of these celebrations, attacking the vice and signs of corruption that were stamped on them in the past. We consider that this respect should be demonstrated both in guaranteeing conditions for these traditions to be freely expressed and to keep them from being used for political or commercial ends. If any Sandinista in the future should disregard this principle we now give notice that he would not be representing the position of the FSLN. Of course, if other political parties or individuals should try to convert popular religious festivals and activities into political acts against the revolution (as has happened in times past), then the FSLN would declare its right to defend the people and the revolution.

*Interpretation of religious issues not a Party function* 6. No Sandinist member in his position as such should give an opinion about the interpretation of religious issues that are under the jurisdiction of the different churches. These questions must be worked out among Christians. If a Sandinista who is also a Christian intervenes in a discussion of this kind he does so as a private individual and as a Christian.

*Divisions in the churches – a matter for Christians* 7. Some reactionary ideologists have accused the FSLN of trying to divide the church. There is nothing more false and ill-intentioned than this accusation. Division in religions is totally alien to the wish and action of the FSLN.

History shows that on important political occasions members of the Catholic church have taken different and even contradictory positions. Along with the Spanish colonizers came the missionaries in order to buttress with the cross the enslavement that the sword had begun. But in opposition to them arose the firmness of Bartolomé de las Casas, the defender of the Indians. At the beginning of the last century there were many priests who fought for the independence of Central America, even to the point of taking up arms. And at the other extreme were priests who with equal vehemence defended the privileges of the Crown in Latin America.

Once liberated from the colonial yoke we find the anti-interventionist position of Bishop Pereira y Castellón calling for the defence of national interests in the face of a United States invasion. During the Somoza era Bishop Calderón y Padilla stands out as a censor of vice, corruption and the Somozas' abuse of power against the common people. And so it has been successively, until the coming of the massive revolutionary commitment which we find today among revolutionary Christians.

We have already mentioned the participation of many Christians in the revolutionary struggle of the people. But we must also say that there were a few like León Pallais and others who were on Somoza's side up to the end.

Let us not forget that in that epoch there were priests who held military rank and government positions – and it should be noted that they were never forced to abandon those positions. But in contrast to those sad examples the notable figure of Gaspar García L. and those of many other Christian Sandinist martyrs stand out.

That situation continues in the present stage. A great majority of Christians support and participate actively in the revolution. But there is also a minority that holds counter-revolutionary political positions. Naturally, Sandinistas are good friends of Christian revolutionaries, but not of the counter-revolutionaries, even though they call themselves Christians. However, the FSLN keeps in communication with the different churches, both at the grassroots and hierarchical levels, without concern for their political positions.

We neither stimulate nor provoke activities to divide the churches.

That is exclusively a matter for Christians and does not pertain to a political organization. If there is division, the churches have to seek causes within themselves and not attribute responsibility to alleged outside evil influences. We are frank in saying that we would look with approval upon an unprejudiced church which would work maturely and responsibly in an increasingly united effort to develop the dialogue and participation that our revolutionary process has opened up.

*Priests in patriotic service* 8. Another matter that has been discussed recently is the participation of priests and religious in the National Reconstruction Government. With regard to this we say that it is the right of all Nicaraguan citizens to participate in the conduct of the country's political affairs, whatever their civil status, and that the Government of National Reconstruction guarantees this right and backs it up by law. Priest *compañeros* who hold government positions in response to the call of the FSLN and their civil obligation have so far performed an extraordinary service.

Our country is confronted with great and difficult problems and in order to go forward it needs the co-operation of every patriot, especially of those who had the chance, denied to most of our people, of receiving a higher education.

Therefore, the FSLN will continue to urge participation in revolutionary tasks by all citizens, lay and religious, whose experience or qualifications are needed for our process. If any religious *compañero* decides to abandon his government responsibilities for personal reasons, that, too, is his right. To exercise one's right to participation and performance of patriotic duty is a matter of personal conscience.

*The lay state represents all citizens* 9. The revolution and the state have different origins, ends and spheres of action from those of religion. For the revolutionary state, religion is a personal matter, incumbent on individuals, churches and the associations that are organized for religious purposes.

The revolutionary state, like every modern state, is a lay state and cannot adopt any religion because it is the representative of all the people – believers and non-believers.

### *Christian Responsibility*

The National Directorate of the Sandinist Front of National Liberation by publishing this official message seeks to clarify the subject in order to help all active revolutionaries of the FSLN and the churches to see their duty and responsibility to reconstruct a country that has been destroyed by 159 years of plunder, repression and dependence. To build Nicaragua's future is a historic challenge that goes beyond our borders and encourages other peoples in their struggle for liberation and integral formation of the new man, and this is a right and a duty of all Nicaraguans, whatever their religious beliefs.

Sandino yesterday, Sandino today, Sandino forever!
A Free Country or Death!

The National Directorate of the
Sandinist Front of National Liberation

# *Notes*

## 1. Conquistadores *and Missionaries – The Evolution of Nation and Church*

1. Jerjez Ruiz and Douglass Sullivan, 'Notes for a History of Protestantism in Nicaragua', unpublished seminar paper (1985) p. 7.
2. Ibid., p. 10.
3. Council for Inter-American Security, 'A New Inter-American Policy for the 80s', Washington 1980.
4. Ibid.
5. Wilton M. Nelson, *El Protestantismo en Centro América*, Editorial Caribe, Miami 1982, p. 16.
6. Ibid., p. 21.
7. John Wilson, 'El Trabajo Morava en Nicaragua', unpublished thesis (1977).
8. Personal interview, February 1986.
9. Personal interview, January 1986.
10. Arturo Parajón and Agustín Ruiz, *1917–1967: 50 Años de Historia Bautista en Nicaragua*, Baptist Convention, Managua 1967.
11. Ruiz and Sullivan, loc. cit., p. 11.
12. Robert Wilson Renouf, *Doing Mission in a Revolutionary World*, USPG 1985, p. 84.
13. Wilson M. Nelson, op. cit., p. 36.
14. Benjamin Cortes, 'La Iglesia Episcopal de Nicaragua', *Amanecer* (Managua) 1985, p. 36.
15. Robert Wilson Renouf, op. cit., p. 88.
16. Benjamin Cortes, loc. cit., p. 37.
17. Robert Wilson Renouf op. cit., p. 107.
18. Ibid., p. 96.
19. Ruiz and Sullivan, loc. cit., p. 8.
20. Wilton M. Nelson, op. cit., p. 66.
21. Carlos Escorcia, 'Las Asambleas de Dios en Nicaragua', *Amanecer* (Managua) December 1985.

22. CEPAD and INDEF (Institute for Basic Evangelism), *Survey of the Protestant Churches in Nicaragua*, Managua 1980.
23. José Miguel Torres, 'What Challenge do the Christian Churches Present to the Revolutionary Process of Nicaragua?', *Fé Cristiana y Revolución Sandinista en Nicaragua*, Historical Institute 1979, p. 145.
24. Wilton M. Nelson, op. cit., p. 48.
25. Ibid., p. 82–3.
26. Ibid., p. 78.
27. Robert Wilson Renouf, op. cit., p. 91.

2. *Challenge and Change – The Protestant Churches since the Revolution*

1. Carlos Escorcia, 'Las Asambleas de Dios en Nicaragua', *Amanacer* (Managua) December 1985, p. 22ff.
2. Interview with Tomás Téllez, 'Los Bautistas en Nicaragua', *Amanacer* (Managua) July 1985, p. 25f.
3. Personal interview, February 1986.
4. Interview with Tomás Téllez, loc. cit., p. 26.
5. Personal interview, March 1986.
6. Robert Wilson Renouf, *Doing Mission in a Revolutionary World*, USPG 1985, p. 97.
7. Personal interview, March 1986.
8. 'The Witness', CEPAD Newsletter 26, April 1986, p. 7.
9. Dorothy Mills Parker, 'The Living Church', US Episcopal Church Magazine, 10 November 1985, p. 6.
10. Jerjez Ruiz and Douglass Sullivan, 'Notes for a History of Protestantism in Nicaragua', unpublished seminar paper (1985) p. 12.
11. Personal Interview, March 1986.
12. Personal interview, February 1986.
13. Personal interview, March 1986.
14. Personal interview, March 1986.
15. Personal interview, March 1986.
16. Deborah Huntington, 'God's Saving Plan', *The Salvation Brokers: Conservative Evangelicals in Central America*, North American Congress on Latin America (NACLA) January-February 1984, p. 28.
17. Ibid., p. 33.
18. Personal interview, February 1986.
19. Personal interview, March 1986.
20. Personal interview, March 1986.

3. *Struggle and Hope – A 'Dawn Theology'*

1. Ernesto Cardenal, *The Gospel in Solentiname*, four vols., Orbis Books 1976–82.

2. Margaret Randall *Christians in the Nicaraguan Revolution*, Vancouver 1983.
3. Cardenal, op. cit., p. 237.
4. Ibid., p. 210.
5. Ibid., p. 191.
6. Ibid., p. 31–2.
7. Ibid., p. 117.
8. 'Analysis and Reflections', *Amanecer* (Managua) October 1983, p. 19.
9. Noel Vargas, 'The Present Aspect of Jesus' Face', *Amanecer* (Managua) October 1983, pp. 19–22.

4. *Engagement and Opposition – Response to Revolution.*

1. Interview with the Permanent Secretary in the Housing Ministry, January 1986.
2. Richard Harris and Carlos M. Vilas (eds), *Nicaragua: A Revolution Under Siege*, Zed Books 1985, p. 10ff.
3. Ibid., chapters three and five.
4. Personal interview, March 1986.
5. Personal interview with Jack Nelson, January 1986.
6. Personal interview, January 1986.
7. '700 Pastors Seek Unity in Week-long Retreat', CEPAD Newsletter, May 1986, p. 1.
8. Ibid., p. 2.
9. CEPAD Annual Report, 1984, p. 6f.
10. CEPAD Newsletter, July 1986, p. 1f. and January 1987, p. 8f.
11. Personal interview, February 1986.
12. Personal interview, March 1986.
13. 'The Ideological Struggle in the Nicaraguan Protestant Churches', *Envio* 15, Central American Historical Institute, September 1982, p. 10ff.
14. Ibid., p. 13.
15. Personal interview, January 1986.
16. Interview, January 1986.
17. Personal interview, March 1986.
18. Teófilo Cabestrero, *Blood of the Innocent: Victims of the Contras' War in Nicaragua*, Orbis/CIIR 1985, p. 1f.
19. 'Massacre in the Mountains', CEPAD Newsletter, August 1986, p. 3.

5. *Struggling for Incarnation – The Theological Battleground*

1. Miguel Casco, 'The Sects in Nicaragua: Heritage of the Past and Instruments of Imperialism', Third Nicaraguan Conference of Social Science, October 1982.

2. 'Christians in Nicaragua's Sandinist Revolution', an official communiqué on religion from the FSLN, October 1980.

3. Teófilo Cabestrero, *Ministers of God, Ministers of the People*, Orbis Books and Zed Press 1983.

4. CEPAD Newsletter, August 1986, p. 7.

5. Personal interview, March 1986.

6. Personal interview, January 1986.

7. Miguel Casco, loc. cit.

8. Ibid.

9. Teófilo Cabestrero, *Blood of the Innocent: Victims of the Contras' War in Nicaragua* Orbis/CIIR 1985, p. 30f., pp. 37–8.

10. Jerjez Ruiz and Douglass Sullivan, 'Notes for a History of Protestantism in Nicaragua', unpublished seminar paper (1985) p. 2.

11. Miguel Casco, loc. cit.

12. Speech to UN Committee on 4 December 1985, by General Vernon Walters (official text).

13. Statement by US Information Service, 7 February 1986.

14. 'The Challenge to Democracy in Central America', US Departments of State and of Defence, June 1986.

15. Speech to Conference on Security and Co-operation in Europe, 2 December 1986, by Ambassador Robert H. Frowick (official text).

16. Letter to Rev. David Haslam, 17 December 1986, from the Public Affairs Office of the US Embassy, London.

17. Ana Maria Ezcurra, *The Vatican and the Reagan Administration*, Neuvomar 1984.

18. Vicky Kemper, 'In the Name of Relief', *Sojourners*, October 1985, p. 13ff.

19. Ibid., p. 17.

20. Deborah Huntington, 'The Prophet Motive', *The Salvation Brokers: Conservative Evangelicals in Central America*, NACLA January-February 1984, p. 3.

21. Ibid., p. 4.

22. Deborah Huntington, 'God's Saving Plan', *The Salvation Brokers: Conservative Evangelicals in Central America*, NACLA January-February 1984, p. 24.

23. Ibid., p. 30.

24. Interview, January 1986.

25. Dianna Melrose, *Nicaragua – The Threat of a Good Example?* Oxfam 1985.

26. Personal interview with an official of the Latin American Council of Churches, January 1986.

27. *Envio*, Vol. 5, No. 49, Central American Historical Institute, July 1986, p. 2ff.
28. Ibid.
29. Ibid.
30. Ibid.
31. Interview, January 1986.

6. *Learning from Nicaragua – A Faith for Today*

1. Personal interview, February 1986.
2. Personal interview, February 1986.
3. Yvonne Dilling (ed.), *What We Have Seen and Heard: The Effects of the Contra War Against Nicaragua*, Witness for Peace 1985.
4. Ed de la Torre, *Touching Ground, Taking Root*, CIIR 1986.

# *Useful Addresses*

Catholic Institute for International Relations, 22 Coleman Fields, London N1 7AF
Central American Human Rights Committee, 83 Margaret Street, London W1N 7HB
CEPAD Newsletter, A. P. 3091, Managua, Nicaragua
Christian Aid, Interchurch House, 35 Lower Marsh, London SE1 7LR
Church Action on Central America, Rev. Peter West, 11 Sulgrave Road, London W6
Nicaraguan Coffee, Traidcraft, Kingsway, Gateshead NE11 0NE
Nicaragua Health Fund, 83 Margaret Street, London W1N 7HB
Nicaragua Solidarity Campaign, 23 Bevenden Street, London N1 6BH
Scottish Aid for Nicaragua, 36 Palmerston Place, Edinburgh EH12 5BJ
Scottish Christians for Nicaragua, 186 Nithsdale Road, Glasgow G41 5QR
Witness for Peace (UK), 4 Larkfield Road, Richmond, Surrey TW9 2PF